The Sailor's Book of the Weather

The Sailor's Book of the Weather

Simon Keeling

John Wiley & Sons, Ltd

Other Wiley Editorial Offices

John Wiley & Sons Inc., 111 River Street, Hoboken, NJ 07030, USA

Jossey-Bass, 989 Market Street, San Francisco, CA 94103-1741, USA

Wiley-VCH Verlag GmbH, Boschstr. 12, D-69469 Weinheim, Germany

John Wiley & Sons Australia Ltd, 42 McDougall Street, Milton, Queensland 4064, Australia

John Wiley & Sons (Asia) Pte Ltd, 2 Clementi Loop #02-01, Jin Xing Distripark, Singapore 129809

John Wiley & Sons Canada Ltd, 22 Worcester Road, Etobicoke, Ontario, Canada, M9W 1L1

Wiley also publishes its books in a variety of electronic formats. Some content that appears in print may
not be available in electronic books.

Library of Congress Cataloging-in-Publication Data

Keeling, Simon.
  The sailor's book of the weather / Simon Keeling.
    p. cm.
  Includes index.
  ISBN 978-0-470-99803-8 (pbk. : alk. paper)
  1. Matine meteorology.   2. Seamanship—Handbooks, manuals, etc.   I. Title.
  QC995.K44 2008
  623.88'8—dc22

                                                    2007050276

British Library Cataloguing in Publication Data

A catalogue record for this book is available from the British Library

ISBN-13: 978-0-470-99803-8

Typeset in 10 on 12 pt Futura regular by SNP Best-set Typesetter Ltd., Hong Kong

Printed and Bound in Spain by Grafos S.A., Barcelona

Contents

Why the Sailor's Book of the Weather?

This may be a question you're asking right now, hopefully not because you think you have wasted your hard-earned money, but because there are lots of weather books out there.

Why is it that I've decided to write down what I think a sailor needs to know and might find useful on-board? Well, it's exactly because *there are* so many weather books for sailors (most of which are very good), but they stretch to many, many pages, often without the result they set out to achieve, that is, an understanding of the weather.

I've structured this book out so that you may dip in or out as and when you need too. It might be that you take the book on-board, or that you keep it on the coffee table at home, or you may even have a copy for both. By the way, please forgive the simplistic drawings, but these are how I visualise the weather.

My hope is that you will find this book useful when you have one of those "How do I find out about that?", or perhaps a "Why is that happening?" type weather question.

Meteorology can seem like a black art with the meteorologist producing forecasts that somehow seem to contradict what you are reading from the charts. While I will not be able to answer all of your questions, I hope to take some of the confusion out of the forecasts.

This book is dedicated to Kathryn, Elizabeth and Daisy for putting up with a husband and daddy as plainly "weather loopy" as me, and for allowing me to spend hours in pursuit of my weather passion. I must also mention my parents for their unfailing support and encouragement; to these people, a special thank you.

Simon Keeling

Introduction to the Weather

Did you know that the phrase "carrying a weight on your shoulders" can be taken more literally than many people think?

Each and every one of us walks around each day with more than 10 tonnes of atmosphere on our shoulders. Humans have evolved to carry such a weight, and that's why, should future generations of humans be born on Mars, they may not be able to travel to Earth because the Martian pressure is far lower than here: they could be crushed! Not that many of us will have to worry about that.

Weight is one thing, gases and chemicals are another. Oxygen makes up 21% of the atmospheric gases, whilst nitrogen accounts for a further 78%. The remaining 1% comprises trace gases including argon, neon, helium, krypton, xenon, carbon dioxide, methane, water vapour and ozone.

The atmosphere sits above our heads extending upwards to a distance in excess of 700 kilometres. The rotation of the earth creates gravity, which keeps the atmosphere in place. The atmosphere is dense at the surface and gets less dense as you head upwards.

The various layers of the atmosphere are shown in the figure below. Many books detail the structure of each of the layers, but I want to keep things fairly simple. Of these layers the most important to us is the troposphere. It is the layer within which we live and within which all weather occurs.

	Exosphere	. . . . ~ 700 km
	↑ ≈ ↓	
	Ionosphere	. . . . ~ 80 km
Stratopause	Mesosphere	. . . . ~ 50 km
Tropopause	Stratosphere	. . . . ~ 10 km
	Troposphere	

The boundary between the troposphere and the next layer, the stratosphere, is called the tropopause; at this point instead of falling with height, temperatures begin to rise. Varying daily and around the world, the tropopause height is higher in warm weather and lower in cold weather.

Heating the Earth

The Earth is heated by the sun. About 6% of incoming radiation is reflected by the atmosphere, 21% is reflected by clouds and 4% is reflected by the Earth's surface. A huge 51% of incoming radiation is absorbed by the land and oceans. The heat we feel each day is actually heat released as radiation by the ground.

About 64% of heat is radiated back to space via the atmosphere and clouds. Around 23% is carried to the clouds and atmosphere by latent heat (see later) in water vapour. The figure below may help.

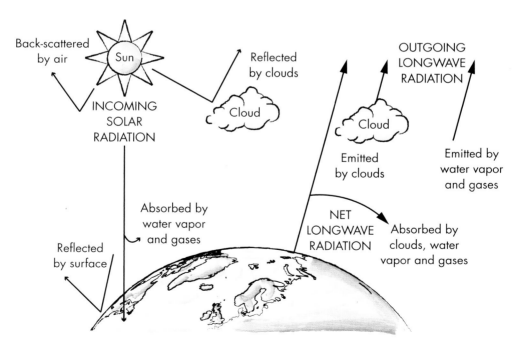

Earth's energy budget

The Seasons

Earth rotates around the sun in an elliptical orbit. As the earth is tilted about its axis, the surface is heated unevenly by the sun throughout the year.

Take 21 December, or the winter solstice. At this time, the sun's rays are shining most directly over the Tropic of Capricorn, with very little shining over the Northern Hemisphere. This is high summer in the Southern Hemisphere, but winter in the north.

By 21 March the sun travels back northwards, and will be shining directly over the equator. The Southern Hemisphere is in autumn, whilst the Northern Hemisphere is looking forward to spring.

On 21 June, the sun shines directly over the Tropic of Cancer in the Northern Hemisphere. It is high summer in the north, whilst the Southern Hemisphere is in the depths of winter.

The 21 September sees autumn through the Northern Hemisphere, with spring coming to the south.

This uneven heating maintains an imbalance and ensures that the Earth's atmosphere, which acts as a fluid, does not achieve equilibrium.

Global Circulation

It is easy to view weather in isolation. You might see a wet day and think, "Why does it rain?" or perhaps experience a frost on a winter's morning and make a mental note of the fern patterns the frost makes on your car.

When forecasting the weather it's important to view these occurrences as part and parcel of the same mechanism. As a forecaster, I view weather charts in 3-D; I don't just look at a single level without taking into account processes taking place at other levels of the atmosphere.

Global circulation is a similar process, in that one process in the atmosphere has a knock-on effect to other happenings. Take a look at the figure overleaf. Although it appears complicated, each one of these processes takes place because of an adjacent phenomenon.

Taking each of the processes in turn:

1. Due to the heating of the sun, warm air rises over the equator or over the area where the sun is shining most directly. This place varies through the year as the sun moves north to south with the seasons. In this zone of rising air, clouds form and it rains. Tropical rain forests are located within this zone.

2. The air moves north and south, eventually cools and sinks back down to earth. As the air sinks, pressure rises, forming the sub-tropical areas of high pressure. For example, in the Azores High, air rotates in a clockwise direction around the high. Some of the surface air returns back to the equator, forming the northeast trade winds. Trade winds from Northern and Southern Hemispheres meet at the Inter-Tropical Convergence Zone. This zone moves north and south with the sun through the year.

3. Other air moves north, blending with cold air from the poles. Where these air masses meet forces air to rise, forming the polar front region.

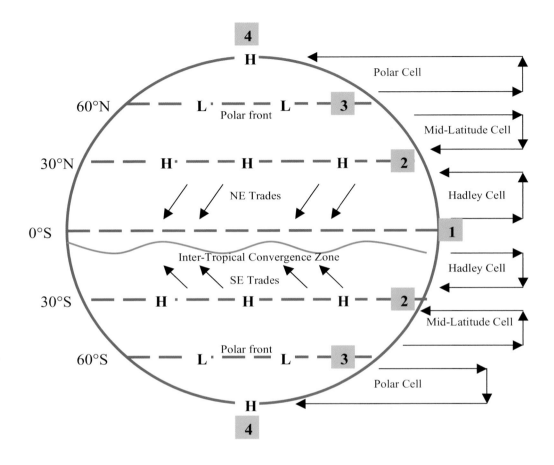

It is also in these zones that we find jet streams at higher levels (see later).

4. Let's now jump to the poles. Here dense, heavy cold air sits at the surface, causing high pressure to form. The cold air drains from the poles into the polar front zone. The air rises, and some returns back to the poles, cools and sinks once again, completing the circulation.

It's important that these circulations are viewed as a whole, not singularly, because one is very much dependent on another.

Physics of the Atmosphere

Physics is important to weather forecasting, as is maths, because they explain numerically the reasons why weather phenomena are occurring. However:

DON'T PANIC!

We all remember maths and physics lessons at school, and let's face it, they weren't exactly inspiring, were they? So, what I intend to tell you in this book is what you need to know.

Remember, there are:

- No confusing equations
- No blackboards
- No tests, and
- No nicking your dinner money!

I have included this section on physics right at the beginning of this book for no other reason than to get it out of the way. It's the subject that when I am running a Weather

School, the merest mention of the word "physics" sends those attending green. So, by getting it out of the way now, it is done and dusted! I hope you agree with this logic.

The Six Principles of Weather Physics

1. What goes up, must come down

Imagine a parcel of air is forced to rise, because it's been heated (a thermal), is forced over a mountain or is lifted along a frontal surface (a bit more complex but I explain this later). This parcel of air has to sink back down to earth somewhere. Rising air is associated with developing weather, clouds and rain, whilst sinking air is associated with higher pressure and better weather.

It went up, so it has to come down!

2. The sun is the ultimate driving force of the weather

The Sun's heating causes imbalances in temperature across the earth's surface. Different surfaces heat up and cool down at different rates. These imbalances create wind and weather.

You'd be nothing without me driving!

3. Cold air is dense, warm air is less dense

Cold air and warm air are a bit like bad friends at a party: they just don't mix. If cold air comes up against warm air, it will dig underneath it. Similarly, when warm air meets colder air it will rise above it. You can think of density in terms of weight. This isn't strictly scientifically correct, but I find it helps. Cold air is heavier than warm air.

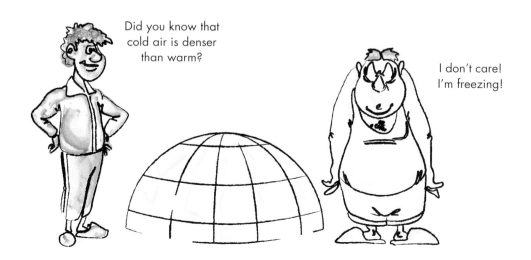

Did you know that cold air is denser than warm?

I don't care! I'm freezing!

4. Air moves from regions of high to low pressure

A vacuum cleaner motor reduces the pressure inside the cleaner. The air outside is under higher pressure and so this air rushes inside the vacuum cleaner when the pressure inside is lowered by turning on the motor. The same principle applies to the weather. Air flows from areas of high to low pressure.

Gonna create me some low pressure!

Low pressure

High pressure

5. Air is a fluid trying to achieve equilibrium

The atmosphere acts as a fluid above our heads. Like any fluid, all the air wants to do is to achieve equilibrium. It wants an easy life and so will take the easy route by flowing from one region to another along the most convenient route. Temperature, mountains, seas and lakes all prevent the air from achieving a balance.

6. Air flows anticlockwise around low pressure and clockwise around high pressure

Visualising where air is flowing on a weather map can help you understand the information the map is trying to portray. I find it useful to draw little chevrons on the isobars (lines of equal pressure shown on a weather chart) as this helps to avoid confusion when you are trying to identify the origins of an air mass.

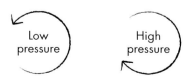

Physical Changes Affecting the Weather

I want you to imagine a parcel of air. This can be anything you like, I tend to think of my parcel as a 1 metre × 1 metre box, but you may think of it as a balloon or anything else you like. Someone once told me they thought of the parcel as an inflatable cow; goodness knows why!

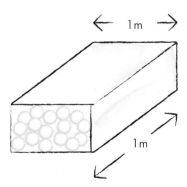

However you imagine your parcel it is on its own, surrounded by the atmosphere, sometimes referred to as "the environment". Our parcel contains air made of the same constituents as the surrounding atmosphere, namely, various gases including water vapour. The molecules which make up the water vapour each contain a certain amount of latent heat (think of latent heat as heat energy trapped within each molecule).

Now any change in the state of the water vapour in our parcel of air (liquid water freezing into ice or heating into vapour) can release or absorb latent heat to or from the surrounding air.

If the change in state is within our parcel alone, then the effect is negligible. However, imagine millions of little air parcels, all containing billions and billions of molecules. If changes take place in all of these parcels, over a substantial area such as an ocean or landmass, then the effect can be large.

Melting will cool a parcel of air.

Phase Changes Cooling a Parcel

Imagine our parcel as being quite happy floating around in the atmosphere.

If the water molecules are below freezing it may be in an ice form. Should the ice melt for some reason, the mechanism which causes the melting of the ice uses some of the heat energy in the molecule. Therefore the net effect is to cool our air parcel.

Not only will melting have the effect of cooling our parcel, but if the water within it were a liquid – that is, a rain drop – and for some reason this evaporated, the overall temperature of the parcel would also cool.

Sublimation may also take place. This is when ice turns directly to vapour without going through a liquid state, and again this would cool our parecl.

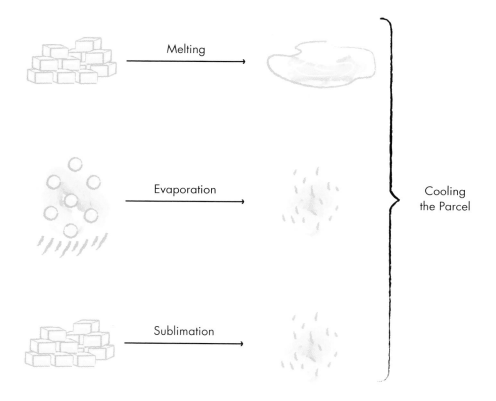

Freezing will warm a parcel of air.

Phase Changes Warming a Parcel

There are also phase changes which act to warm our parcel of air, and unsurprisingly, these are the opposite of the changes cooling a parcel.

If the water vapour in our parcel were to condense out, let's say in the form of a cloud droplet, a certain amount of latent heat would be released by this process, thus warming our parcel slightly.

Finally, deposition – that is, the process of vapour turning directly to ice without going through a liquid phase – brings about the same resultant warming.

Once again, remember that the effect of a change in phase of a single droplet is small, but if this change happens many, many times, then the result can be large.

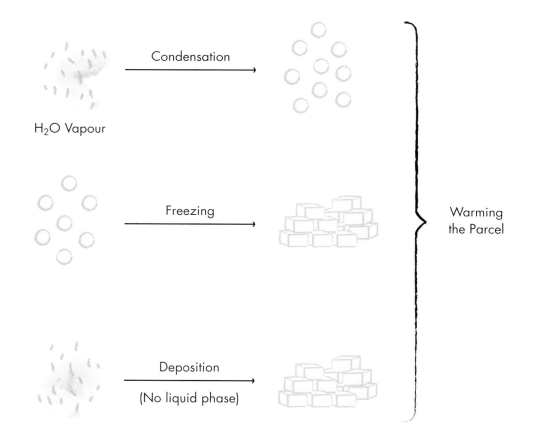

H$_2$O Vapour

Condensation

Freezing

Deposition
(No liquid phase)

Warming
the Parcel

The Rise and Fall of an Air Parcel: Stability

Next I want you to think about how temperature changes within our air parcel can affect it in relation to the surrounding air. Do you remember we said how warm air was less dense than cold air? Okay, let's apply this to our air parcel.

Now, first of all we have to make an assumption here, and that is that no air is being exchanged between the air parcel and the surrounding air. We also assume that no heating of the parcel is taking place. We call this an "adiabatic process". Adiabatic literally means the absence of heat transfer. This is a bit technical, but it is an important assumption to make.

As air rises, it expands and cools. The reason for this expansion is that as you go higher in the atmosphere the less dense the surrounding air is, and so anything travelling in it has a tendency to expand. Similarly, a balloon, with less pressure exerted on its exterior, would expand as it rose through the atmosphere.

Now, our air parcel could be dry (all the water within it is in a vapour form) or it may be saturated (all the water vapour has condensed into a liquid).

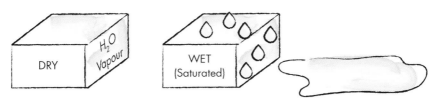

In dry air, the temperature decreases by 10°C per kilometre.

If the Parcel Is Dry...

Imagine a dry parcel of air is forced to rise for some reason. That may be because of a mountain range, heating from the sun, or perhaps the slope of a front (see later).

As our parcel rises, it will cool and expand. The rate of this cooling is always the same at around 10°C per kilometre.

This rate of temperature decrease with height is known as the dry adiabatic lapse rate. "Lapse rate" describes the decrease in temperature with height.

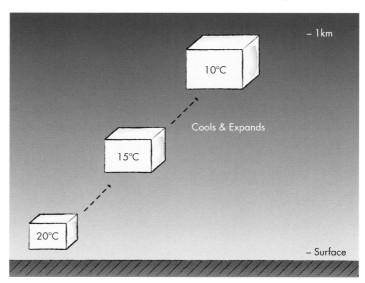

In saturated (wet) air the temperature decreases at about 6°C per kilometre.

If the Parcel Is Wet (Saturated) . . .

Let's say that the water inside our parcel is in the process of or has condensed. We know that the condensation process releases latent heat.

Now, that release of latent heat will warm our parcel and therefore reduce its lapse rate, by about 4°C per kilometre. So, instead of a lapse rate of 10°C per kilometre, it is now around 6°C per kilometre (although this is dependent on the amount of water vapour and condensation taking place).

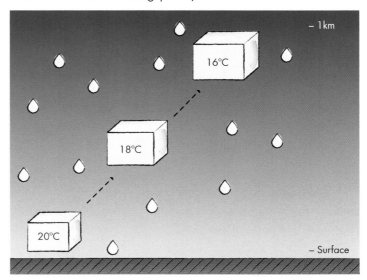

Stability of the Atmosphere

Think about our parcel of air being warmed. Remember that warm air is less dense, and more buoyant, than cold air. So, if our parcel becomes warmer and more buoyant than its surroundings, it will start to rise.

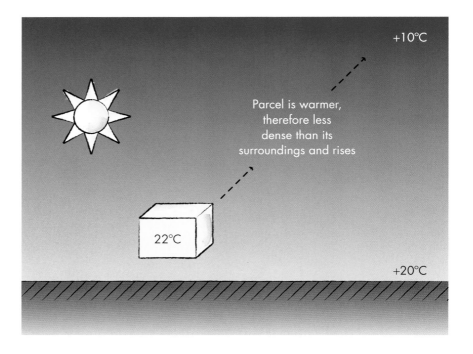

Should the opposite occur, and our parcel of air be cooled (perhaps by a melting ice or evaporation), then the parcel becomes more dense and less buoyant. The result is that the parcel sinks.

Now, I want you to think about the temperature of the surrounding air ("the environment") and how this could influence our air parcel.

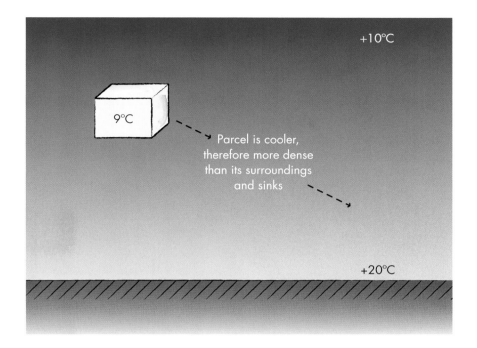

If the surrounding air is cooler and more dense than the air parcel, what happens to the parcel when it is warmed and cooled, respectively?

Likewise, what happens if the environment is warmer and less dense than the parcel?

Stable Air

Stable air can be misinterpreted as giving fine, settled conditions. This is not always the case; for example, the warm sector of a frontal system is considered stable.

Instead, the stability of the air relates to the motions that can take place within it, rather than the weather, although I have to admit that unstable does generally mean mixed conditions.

Let me show you what I mean.

In stable air, if our parcel were forced upwards, it would cool faster than the environment around it, become more dense and then sink back to its original level.

Or, if it were forced downwards, then it would become warmer, less dense and then rise back to its original level.

It's best to understand this from a diagram. The figure on the facing page shows the various stages of a parcel being warmed, or cooled, in relation to the temperature of the surrounding air.

You can see that in both cases the parcel of air has a tendency to sink, or rise, back to its starting point.

A good example of a cloud resulting from stable air is a stratocumulus cloud. The cloud can be seen to have "rolls" in it as the air parcels have risen and sunk, condensing and evaporating before achieving near temperature equilibrium.

Stratocumulus clouds indicates stable air.

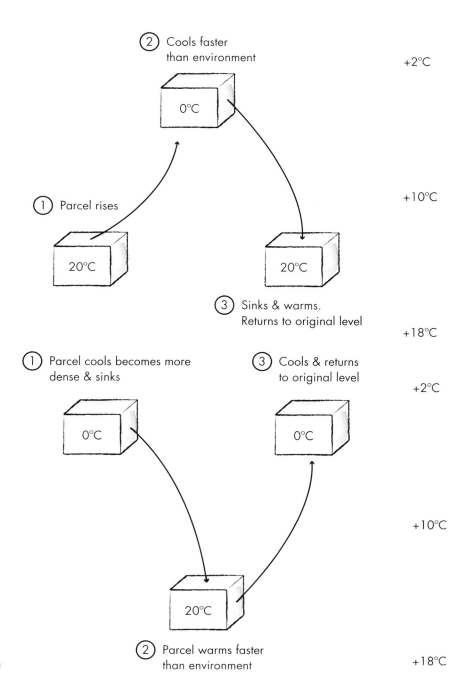

(2) Cools faster
than environment

+2°C

(1) Parcel rises

+10°C

0°C

20°C

20°C

(3) Sinks & warms.
Returns to original level

+18°C

(1) Parcel cools becomes more
dense & sinks

(3) Cools & returns
to original level

+2°C

0°C

0°C

(2) Parcel warms faster
than environment

+10°C

20°C

Stable air

+18°C

23

Unstable Air

Unstable air is air which can lead to the formation of precipitation, such as showers.

Imagine that our air parcel is forced upwards. If for some reason the air parcel finds itself warmer than the air surrounding it, it will remain buoyant and will continue to rise.

So, why could it be warmer? It may be due to the surrounding air becoming much colder; perhaps by colder air moving in from elsewhere (known as "cold air advection").

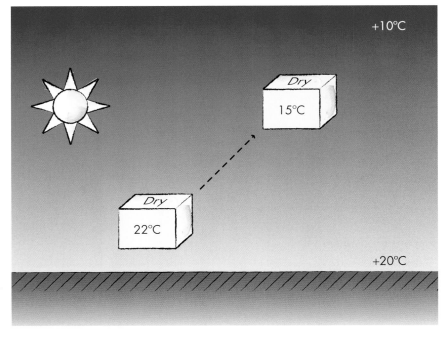

If a parcel of air is dry, in an unstable air mass, it will rise, but no clouds are seen.

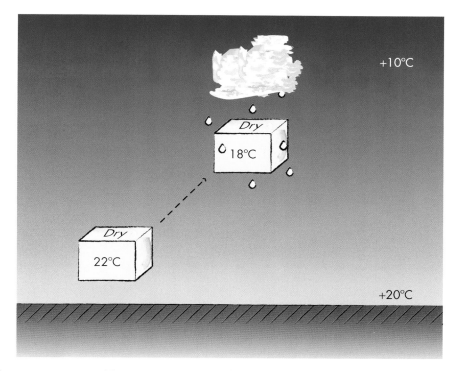

If a parcel is wet, in an unstable air mass, vapour will condense and form clouds.

Another possibility is that as the air parcel is rising the water vapour in it is condensing. Remember that the condensation process has a warming affect (therefore slows down the lapse rate).

You can see this process taking place on a day when cumulus clouds are in the air. The sky may start out perfectly blue, but shortly after sunrise flecks of cumulus can be seen. These continue to grow until large clouds are formed. Showers may begin to fall.

Cumulus clouds show the air is unstable.

Cumulus and cumulonimbus clouds are indicative of an unstable atmosphere.

Cumulus   Cumulonimbus

Atmospheric Forces

The movement of the atmosphere is controlled by various forces acting upon it. The interaction of these forces assists in the creation of phenomena such as the wind.

The forces to consider are:

- Pressure gradient force

- Coriolis force

- Centrifugal force

- Friction

I will deal with each of these forces in turn. Please do not panic if you don't quite understand how each individual force works! The main point I am trying to get across in the next few pages is that the forces act together, and in doing so create certain aspects of the weather.

Pressure Gradient Force

We already know from our six principles that air flows from high to low pressure, and this is the pressure gradient force.

If there were no other forces on the earth, air would flow straight from areas of high to low pressure.

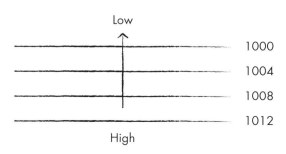

Rik Andes

Coriolis Force

The Coriolis force is an apparent force that acts upon pressure systems as they move across the Earth's surface. It acts to deflect objects to the right in the Northern Hemisphere and to the left in the Southern Hemisphere.

The best way to imagine the Coriolis force is to think back to when you were a child. Do you remember those roundabouts that you stood on whilst your friend pushed the roundabout? If you jumped off and traced your route, you would not jump in a straight line but would appear to be deflected. This is the same as the Coriolis force.

The Coriolis force is strongest at the poles and zero at the equator.

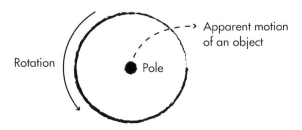

Centrifugal Force

Have you ever watched clothes in a washing machine as it begins a spin cycle? What happens? The clothes get "squeezed" to the edge of the washing machine drum, being forced out from the centre by the rotation of the drum. This is centrifugal force.

Centrifugal force is an apparent force that deflects particles (in this case winds) away from the centre of a rotation. And what in weather rotates? Low and high pressure, of course, with centrifugal force apparently making air want to escape from the rotating centre of these systems.

Friction

Friction is the final force to be reckoned with. It is best to think of friction as a brake. It opposes motion and is always opposite to the direction of that motion.

Friction can be caused by many things, but when thinking about the weather it's best to imagine it caused by buildings, trees, mountains or even the sea.

Think for a moment. If the land surface is rougher than the sea, then friction will have more effect inland than at sea. Therefore, winds are less over land than at sea.

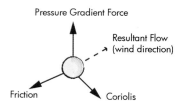

By combining forces a resultant flow is created. It is this flow we feel as the wind.

Workings of the Weather

Air Masses

It's always nice to know people's background, isn't it? After all, when you go for an interview, your prospective employer would like to see your C.V. in order to get an idea about you and your previous experience.

In the same way, it is nice to know the origins of the air that is above our heads. If you know where it has come from, you can make a more accurate assessment of what the weather is likely to be doing in the future.

One of the easiest ways of forecasting is to identify the air mass that is affecting you, and then ask yourself why the weather may not fit with the definition of that air mass type. You can then amend your forecast accordingly.

Think of an air mass as a block of air. If this block is stuck over one area for any length of time, it will tend to take on the characteristics of the surface that it is over.

An air mass is defined as "a body of air, with a similar temperature throughout, separated from an adjacent body by a sharp transition zone (i.e. a front)".

The main classifications of air masses are:

Tropical air masses are warm and moist.

- Tropical

- Continental

- Polar

- Maritime

- Equatorial

Continental air is dry.

Polar air masses often bring snow showers and bright skies.

Maritime air is wet.

What weather is implied by these names and what do you think the weather is going to be like with each one? It's pretty self explanatory, really: tropical is warm, continental dry, polar cold, maritime wet, and equatorial hot.

Air masses can also be combined. For example, if the block of air moves away from its region of origin, it will become what is known as "modified". Take, for example, a block of air in the tropical regions, passing northeastwards over the Atlantic Ocean. As it moves over the ocean it becomes a tropical maritime air mass, which is warm and wet.

The main air masses affecting the British Isles are:

- Tropical maritime
- Polar maritime
- Tropical continental

- Polar continental
- Arctic maritime
- Returning polar maritime

Each of these brings its own type of weather, and we'll take a look at each one in turn.

Characteristics of Air Masses

	Tropical maritime		Polar maritime		Tropical continental	
	Summer	*Winter*	*Summer*	*Winter*	*Summer*	*Winter*
Temperature	Mild to warm and muggy	Mild	Cool	Cold	Hot	Depends on wind
Visibility	Poor on western and southern coasts	Poor on western and southern coasts	Good, moderate in showers	Good, moderate in showers, poor in wintry showers	Good but may be poor in east	Good but may be poor in east
Weather	Drizzle, mist, fog, low cloud on western coasts. Drier inland	Drizzle, mist, fog, low cloud on western coasts. Drier inland	Sunny spells and showers	Sunny spells and showers, some wintry	Sunny, risk of fog in east. Thunderstorms in west	Sunny spells. Risk of fog patches in east.

	Polar continental		Arctic maritime		Returning polar maritime	
	Summer	*Winter*	*Summer*	*Winter*	*Summer*	*Winter*
Temperature	Cool	Cold	Cool	Very cold	Mild	Mild
Visibility	Very good but moderate in showers	Very good but moderate or poor in showers	Good but moderate in showers	Good but poor in showers in east	Good but poor in showers	Good but poor in showers
Weather	Showers in north and west	Showers, wintry in north and west	Showers in east	Wintry showers in east	Heavy showers	Heavy showers

Tropical Maritime

This type of air mass is the most frequent visitor to UK shores, brought along by a southwest wind. Air originates over the tropical regions of the Atlantic and is transported northeastwards. As it passes over cooler water on its journey north, the air picks up moisture from the sea surface. This results in low cloud, drizzle and fog along western and southern coasts of the UK and Ireland. However, it is frequently warm, so areas protected from the southwest wind by high ground (such as the Midlands, northeast England and eastern Scotland) can have pleasant, warm, sunny days.

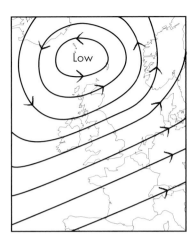

Polar Maritime

This air mass originates at the poles, before passing over the cool Atlantic northwest of the UK. Because the cold air passes over a warmer sea, it is unstable, and this creates showers. The showers can be heavy and frequent around western and northern coasts. Severe frosts can occur overnight away from the coasts. Visibility is excellent out of the showers.

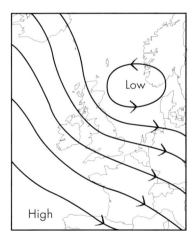

Tropical Continental

During the summer months, the tropical continental air mass is generally hot and dry as the air dries out during its journey over the European landmass. The arrival of this air mass brings high temperatures in summer and fairly warm days in the winter. However, watch for thunderstorms in the summer months as colder air moves in at upper levels off the Atlantic, creating instability. There may also be fog patches in the Channel and along eastern coasts.

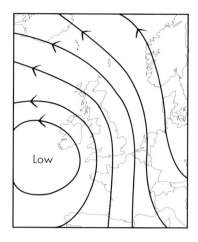

Polar Continental

Originating at the north pole, air flows over the cold landmass of northern Russia, passing over Scandinavia or Eastern Europe and eventually reaching the shores of the United Kingdom. The sea track is short, so moisture is limited and the air mass tends to be dry, but bitterly cold in winter. Eastern coasts may have drizzle or snow pellets in the winter, with murky conditions spreading inland. Western coasts are usually brighter with sunny spells and dry.

Visibility may be poor in the east but better in the west.

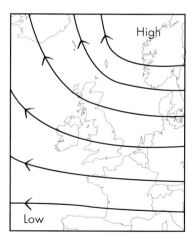

Arctic Maritime

Mainly visiting during the winter months, arctic maritime air can be very cold. It flows over the frozen Arctic Sea north of the United Kingdom. It is so cold that it can hold little water vapour, and so precipitation is in the form of showers, most of them wintry. Because the wind comes from the north or northeast, the first places the showers arrive are northern and eastern Scotland, together with eastern England. Visibility is usually good with crystal clear skies away from eastern coasts.

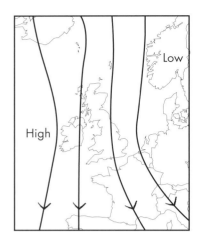

Returning Polar Maritime

The returning polar maritime air mass is caused by low pressure southwest of Ireland. As air flows from the poles over the Atlantic it is forced southwards, often as far as the Azores. This air then passes northeastwards, bringing deeply unstable air over the British Isles. Showers are often frequent and heavy in this air mass, with these merging into longer spells of rain. Take care not to confuse returning polar maritime with tropical maritime air.

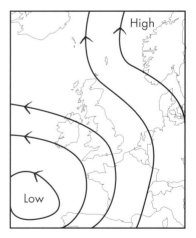

Pressure Systems

Probably the most recognisable feature of a weather chart is the areas of high and low pressure marked on it. Isobars drawn on the chart join places of equal atmospheric pressure.

As a rule of thumb, low pressure brings poor weather and strong winds, whilst high pressure may give fair conditions with lighter winds. However, anyone who has been exposed to the weather for any length of time soon comes to realise that these definitions are somewhat loose.

In this section I want to look at how high and low pressure forms.

First, though, a reminder: winds flow in an anticlockwise direction around low pressure and in a clockwise direction around high pressure.

It's also useful to familiarise oneself with how hurricane and tropical storms are depicted on surface charts.

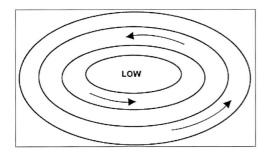

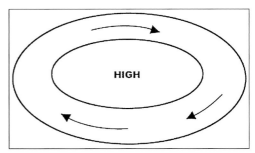

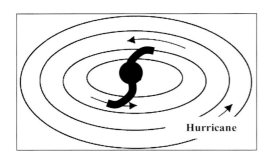

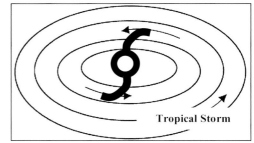

High Pressure

I always imagine the formation of pressure systems as a logical sequence. This way I remember the process more easily, so I hope this will be useful for you as well.

High pressure forms as:

1. Air converges aloft, forcing air to sink (or subside) and preventing the formation of cloud.

2. As the air reaches the surface it cannot travel through the ground, and so therefore it spreads out, or to put it technically, diverges.

3. The diverging air flows to regions of lower pressure (remember the fourth principle, "air flows from high to low pressure").

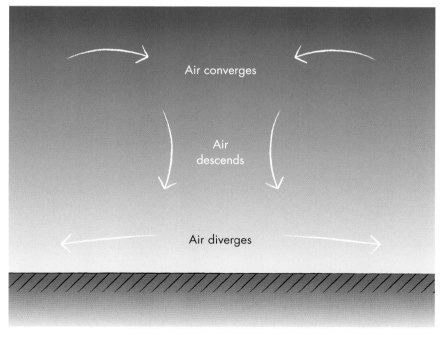

Formation of high pressure

High Pressure Weather

There are two types of high pressure system, cold and warm.

Cold Highs

The cold high frequently forms over the landmass of eastern Europe during the winter months. Cold, dense air sits over the ground, increasing pressure. Any warm air that tries to invade gets forced to rise above the cold air, effectively trapping it at the surface.

The high tends to break down only when warm air mixes with the colder air and the surface layer "warms through". This can take some time.

The weather underneath cold areas of high pressure is usually settled with calm winds. It can be that the high starts off with clear skies.

Visibility usually falls and mist and fog can form.

As warmer air spreads in aloft, a layer of moist air and pollution can get trapped. This allows cloud to form, acting as a "lid" on the air below. Conditions frequently stagnate with little change for days on end.

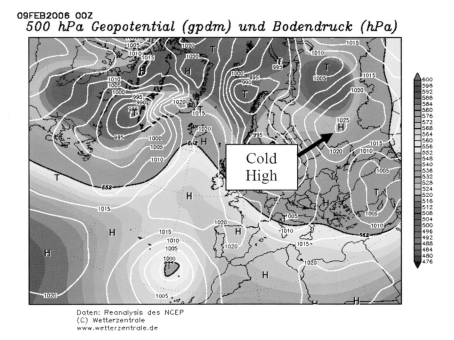

A cold high centred over eastern Europe

Warm Highs

These are the highs we find close to the coasts of western Europe. They typically form as warm air gets pumped northeastwards across the Atlantic.

Think of the air above our heads as a column stretching to the tropopause (below which level all weather occurs). The height of the tropopause varies daily dependent on temperature. As the warm air is pushed northwards and slows down, a large column of air builds above our heads. It increases pressure at the surface and brings the warm high. The map below shows the warm air pushing north (depicted by the red arrows) and high pressure building at the surface as a result.

This usually decays as colder air, usually from the west, undercuts the warm column, disrupting the surface high and reintroducing more unsettled conditions.

43

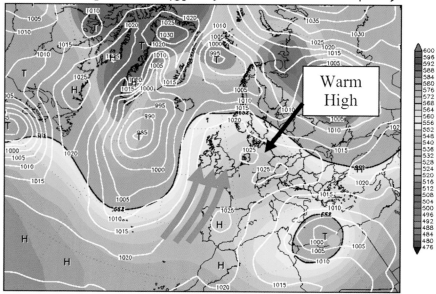

01FEB2006 00Z
500 hPa Geopotential (gpdm) und Bodendruck (hPa)

Warm
High

Daten: Reanalysis des NCEP
(C) Wetterzentrale
www.wetterzentrale.de

A warm high centred over western and central Europe

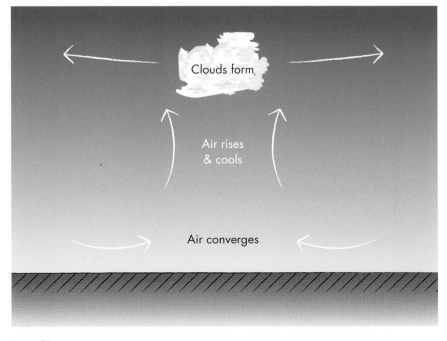

Formation of low pressure

Nimbostratus brings rain on a warm front.

Low Pressure Weather

Unsettled weather is frequently associated with low pressure, and this is indeed true of most areas of low pressure, especially in the winter months.

Frontal systems around low pressure are frequently responsible for the rain; later we discuss in more detail the weather associated with each of these.

One thing to bear in mind is that close to the centre of an area of low pressure the weather can be quite pleasant. Light winds and clear skies can bring beautiful days, and one might wonder whether one is really so close to low pressure.

It is also worth remembering that as well as the more familiar polar front low (the type that usually move in from the Atlantic) there are other types of low, such as the heat low.

The heat low forms during the summer months when land surfaces are heated. The heated air rises and therefore pressure falls at the surface. Air rushes in from outside the low to replace that being lost, often enhancing the sea breeze effect (discussed later).

The rising air associated with the heat low may be sufficient to trigger heavy showers or thunderstorms inland.

Buys-Ballot's Law

A very useful way to locate low pressure is using Buys-Ballot's Law. This states that if you stand with your back to the wind, low pressure will always be on your left (in the Northern Hemisphere). This can also be useful when assessing whether a heavy shower is likely to ease soon.

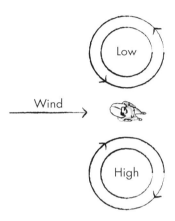

Fronts

When you see weather charts on the television, and often on the Internet, they usually have fronts marked on them. My neighbour (Bob) hates the phrase "weather front" as he says that all fronts are associated with weather, and I have to admit to agreeing with him. So in this section, I will just stick to the word "fronts".

There are four main types of front usually marked on weather charts:

1. Warm front: where warmer air displaces colder air

2. Cold front: where colder air displaces warmer air

3. Occluded front: where the cold front has caught up with the warm front and lifted the warm air above the surface of the ground

4. Trough: similar in characteristics to a cold front and usually denoted on a chart as an area of increased showery activity. However, don't confuse this with a tropical trough, or easterly wave.

Identifying fronts is easier in temperate and polar regions, but harder in the tropics.

Warm fronts are denoted by semi-circles, sometimes coloured red on charts. Cold fronts are shown by triangles, sometimes coloured blue, whilst an occlusion is shown by alternating semi-circles and triangles, sometimes coloured purple. Troughs are shown either as solid or broken black lines.

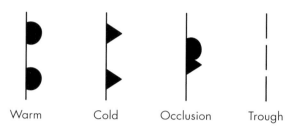

Warm   Cold   Occlusion   Trough

Warm, cold, occlusion and trough fronts on a surface weather chart

Direction of Movement of the Front

The direction in which the front is moving is shown by the direction in which the triangles or semi-circles are pointing.

Should the symbols be shown on alternating sides of the frontal line, this means that the front is stationary at that point.

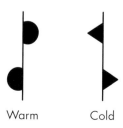

Warm   Cold

Stationary fronts

Further Classification of Fronts

Fronts can be further classified to show whether there is significant weakening or strengthening of the front taking place. These classifications seem to be used only on the charts originating from the UK Meteorological Office. They are:

1. Ana fronts: These are developing fronts where air is mainly ascending, marked on some charts by "−" symbols along the main frontal line. This process is know as frontogenesis and means the generation of a new front or the regeneration of an old one.

2. Kata fronts: These fronts are weakening, dying fronts. The kata front is shown by a "+" along the main frontal line. The kata front process is know as frontolysis.

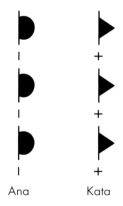

Ana   Kata

Ana and kata fronts

Upper Air Fronts

Once again, mainly marked on charts issued by the UK Meteorological Office, upper air fronts are shown in the same way as surface fronts. However, one major difference exists: on an upper air front, the triangles or semi-circles are not solid.

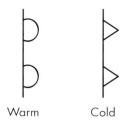

Warm   Cold

Warm and cold fronts above the surface

Warm Fronts

As its name suggests, a warm front marks the boundary between a cooler and a warmer air mass. In the British Isles the air mass bringing the warmer weather is usually tropical maritime or tropical continental.

When watching for a warm front, things to look out for include:

1. High level cirrus cloud, which often heralds the approach of the warm front.

2. Cirrus thickens to cirrostratus and then altostratus. Winds will back.

Cirrus and cirrostratus clouds are first indication of the approach of a warm front.

Altostratus often produce halos, confirming the approach of the warm front.

3. Rain usually begins to fall as the sun or moon disappears behind the altostratus cloud.

4. Cloud then continues to thicken into nimbostratus, with rain becoming more persistent.

(During steps 1 to 4 the winds will be backing and freshening, whilst the pressure will fall.)

5. As the front passes, the rain turns more to drizzle and visibility deteriorates. Temperature rises, wind veers.

6. Warm sector conditions prevail, often bringing poor visibility, drizzle and stratus cloud.

It's often easier to view fronts and the effects of the weather as they pass as a diagram. Remember, though, that each front is different and may not conform to this idealised model.

It's easy to see from the diagram how the warm front works. As the less dense, warm air meets the denser, cold air ahead of the front, it is forced to rise

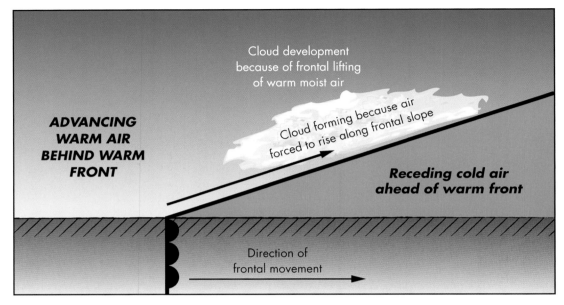

Cloud development
because of frontal lifting
of warm moist air

Cloud forming because air
forced to rise along frontal slope

ADVANCING
WARM AIR
BEHIND WARM
FRONT

Receding cold air
ahead of warm front

Direction of
frontal movement

Cross section of a warm front

and "slides" up the colder air, until eventually the colder air gives way and the warm front passes.

WARM FRONT	Ahead of the front	At the front	Behind the front
Wind	Backs and increases	Veers and is gusty	Becomes steady, may back slightly
Pressure	Falls steadily	Falls.	Steady
Temperature	Begins to rise	Rising more quickly	Rises quickly
Cloud	Increases, lowers and thickens	Thick and low base	Low but may break
Rainfall	Rain as sun or moon disappear	Becomes heavy and is continuous	Drizzle; may stop away from coast
Visibility	Good, then moderate, poor near front	Moderate or poor in rain	Moderate or poor; often mist or fog at sea breaks

Watch for darkening clouds and squalls as the cold front approaches.

Cold Fronts

Cold fronts usually follow behind warm fronts and replace the warm air (generally tropical maritime) with colder, denser air (frequently polar maritime).

Here's what happens when a cold front approaches.

1. Cloud thickens and any drizzle in the warm sector starts to become more persistent.

2. The winds increase and become gusty.

3. Rain may become heavy.

4. As the front passes, there is a risk of thunderstorms.

(During steps 1 to 3 the wind direction will be fairly steady, although will back by step 4.)

After the cold front passes:

5. Clearer skies may follow.

6. Cumulus clouds and showers often develop within 1 to 3 hours.

Once the cold front has passed, cumulus will form, bringing showers.

(At step 5 the winds may veer sharply and be squally, then they may back at step 6.)

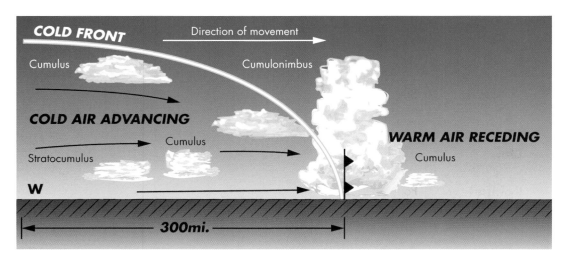

COLD FRONT   Direction of movement

Cumulus   Cumulonimbus

COLD AIR ADVANCING   **WARM AIR RECEDING**

Cumulus

Stratocumulus   Cumulus

W

300mi.

Cross section of a cold front

Paul Albertella

Once again, remember that fronts rarely conform to an idealised model and each one is different. What I have described above is merely the "perfect" front, and although it may happen in real life, there will be day-to-day differences.

COLD FRONT	*Ahead of the front*	*At the front*	*Behind the front*
Wind	Steady (warm sector conditions)	Gusty, possibly squally; backs sharply	Veers sharply, gusty winds.
Pressure	Steady, begins to fall close to front.	Falls then rises rapidly	Rises
Temperature	Steady, mild	Sharp drop	Falls
Cloud	Increases close to front	Low and thick	Clear for a time, then cumulus
Rainfall	Possible drizzle then rain close to front	Heavy, possibly squally; risk of thunder	Showers after 1 to 2 hours
Visibility	Moderate or poor	Moderate or poor in rain	Good

Occluded Fronts

The occluded front occurs at the point where the cold and warm fronts meet. There are two types of occluded front: warm and cold.

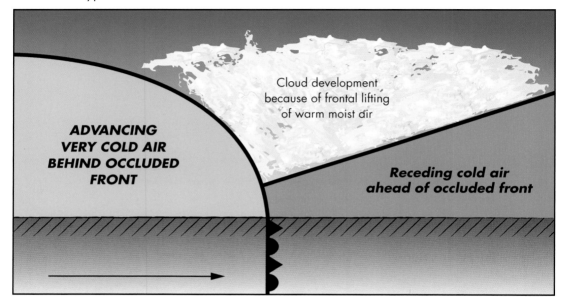

Cross section of an occluded front

Cold occlusions are most common and occur where the air following the front is colder and denser and cuts underneath the cool air ahead of the front. The resultant conditions are similar to those experienced along a cold front.

Seen in 3-D the front shows a "wedge" of warm air which has been lifted above the surface.

A warm occluded front occurs where warmer air meets colder air. The warmer air rises above the colder air, in much the same way as a warm front. Conditions are often similar to a warm front.

Troughs

A trough is identified on a surface chart by a solid black line or on American charts by a dashed line. The trough indicates an area of enhanced showery activity, and one can usually identify it by a dip in the isobars.

Increasing cumulus after clear skies indicate an approaching trough.

The tell-tale signs of a trough are:

1. A spell of an hour or so of fine weather ahead of the trough.

2. Rapidly increasing cloud, usually cumulus.

3. A period of showery rain, sometimes heavy. Hail and thunder may appear, with squally winds. The rain usually lasts less than an hour.

4. Clearance is equally rapid, often to clear skies as a ridge builds behind the trough.

5. The more vigorous the trough (i.e. the heavier the showers), the higher the chance of several hours of fine weather behind it.

If you are planning to sail in tropical regions, such as crossing the Atlantic, troughs may be called tropical waves. These may develop into tropical storms or hurricanes and are clearly seen on satellite pictures as bands of showers pushing west with the trade winds.

If you get caught by a tropical wave, you know about it! When forecasting for Atlantic crossings we regularly get reports of 60 knot wind gusts from such troughs, together with heavy thundershowers.

The Polar Front Low

You will remember that a front marks the boundary of two air masses, containing air of different temperature, moisture content and, therefore, density.

This mixture creates a substantial amount of turbulence and instability at the point where the two air masses meet. Adding in the Coriolis effect provides a point around which the air begins to rotate.

In this section I want to take you through the five stages in the life of a depression as it would form along the polar front; that's the boundary line where cold air from the poles meets warmer air from the equator and is the front that most often affects the coasts of Europe.

Stage 1: Birth

- Atmosphere is near equilibrium with cold air to the north and warm air to the south

Stage 2: Growing up

- A perturbation upsets the balance of warm and cold air, shifting cold air south and warm air north

- The result is an open shallow wave depression

- Depressions moves quickly in direction of warm sector isobars

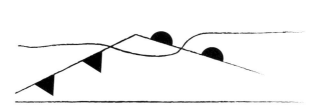

Stage 3: Adolescence

- The low pressure begins to swirl

- The cold front moves faster than the warm front

- "Swirling" becomes self-supporting

- Depression starts to slow down

Stage 4: Maturity

- Low pressure area deepens further

- The cold front catches up with the warm front, lifting warm air above the surface and forming the occluded front

- Depression is now slower moving

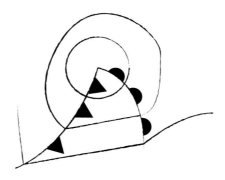

Stage 5: Old age

- Occluding process is well under way

- Depression becomes very slow-moving or stationary

- Depression weakens as its source air becomes cut off

The Jet Stream

If you have been on a long-haul flight you may well have heard the pilot talking about the "jet stream". Often, he or she will refer to a tail-wind or a head-wind and

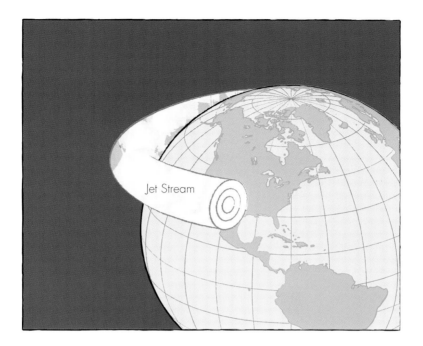

Jet Stream

may say that "we have made up time because the tail-winds were favourable". Well, more often than not, those winds are actually caused by the jet stream.

As fast-moving tubes of air (wind speeds over 200 knots have been recorded), high in the atmosphere, jet streams occur at between 25,000 and 35,000 feet, just under the tropopause. The largest jet streams flow from west to east in both the Northern and Southern Hemispheres. On the way across the Atlantic from Europe to the United States, pilots try to avoid the jet stream as this gives head winds. But on the way back, pilots will try to find them as they can blow the aircraft along and save fuel.

Jet streams don't occur as one continuous tube of winds, they tend to meander around the world. They can break in places and are part of the mechanism responsible for the formation of high and low pressure systems. A forecaster will watch the charts for places where a jet stream strengthens or weakens, as this can identify areas where such pressure systems may develop or weaken rapidly.

The jet stream usually occurring between about 40°N and 70°N, and 40°S and 70°S, is referred to as the polar jet. Closer to the equator there is a more minor jet stream called the sub-tropical jet occurring between about 20 and 50°. During the summer months yet another jet stream occurs close to the equator, called the equatorial easterly jet, and it is this one to watch closely for the development of hurricanes and also in forecasting the Asian monsoons.

This book deals with surface meteorology, and so, for now, that is all that I will say on the subject of jet streams, but there are many good books out there which will tell you more.

Practical Forecasting

Plotted Weather Charts and Forecasting

This is a skill that is being rapidly lost as computers replace humans in the field of weather forecasting. Undoubtedly, computers are very useful for performing mass calculations and producing some wonderful numerical weather predictions. Computers are also useful in analysing charts, especially in the placement of isobars.

However, what computers cannot do as well as a human is spot an erroneous observation or read more meaning into a chart.

Analysis of observations and the placing of fronts is a real skill. Given time and patience this skill can be put to great use and can help when forecasting the weather.

There are many good books which show how to draw up charts using information that you may hear on the Shipping and Inshore Waters radio (and Internet) forecast. Unfortunately, coastal station reports are now included only in the

0045 hrs and 0550 hrs bulletins. However, if you can get used to plotting charts and analysing them, you will not need to depend on other forecasts and will have a skill to use in the future.

Analysis gets you into the 3-D pattern of weather. As you draw up the charts and observe the surrounding conditions, you learn what to include in your assessment of the area of interest.

There are now alternatives available, notably charts that are produced hourly via the Internet. These often plot surface observations and then overlay computer-drawn isobars. One such hourly chart for the British Isles is at http://meteocentre.com/analyse/map.php?map=UK.

A sample of a map is shown overleaf.

The chart shows surface observations. Each observation is plotted around a central station circle. This circle is filled in depending upon how much cloud there is in the sky. Emanating from the circle is a stick; this points in the direction from which the wind is coming from. Attached to the stick are feathers indicating the the wind speed. A full feather represents 10 knots, a half-feather 5 knots.

On the top left, the number in red is the air temperature. Following the observation clockwise, the next three-digit number represents air pressure in millibars and tenths; the number displayed is the last three digits. For example, "159" represents 1015.9 millibars.

Underneath this (if available) is the pressure tendency in the preceding three hours, both in tenths of a millibar (e.g., "20" would indicate a change of two millibars) and a small pictorial diagram to show whether pressure was falling, rising or steady.

Following the circle around, you will come to a figure in green. This is the dew point. The closer the dew point to the temperature, the more moist the air is.

And finally, if there is any weather occurring at the time the observation is made, this is marked between the dew point and temperature. Visibility may sometimes be marked to the left of the present weather symbol.

A sample of the station plot is shown in on page 72. Of course, what these plots don't do is draw on the fronts. This is down to you.

Using the techniques of recognising fronts, it should be possible to start drawing on the fronts. At first you might be, well, hopeless at it. But with time, your technique will improve.

http://meteocentre.com/toulouse/ **For non-commercial use ONLY**
Surface plot stc/070119/1300 / upa/070119/00

Of course, there is nothing like watching an expert analyse a chart and then copying their methods. We can't do that here, but what I can do is to give you a step-by-step guide to drawing on the fronts.

1. Print out the hourly analysis map from a site such as Meteocentre.

2. Lightly sketch in where you think fronts might be. Remember to use the information about fronts, such as: they indicate two air masses, there is likely to be a marked temperature change across the front, pressure usually rises behind a front, and the wind will change direction.

3. Print out an official frontal analysis chart from www.weatheronline. co.uk, www.wetterzentrale.de or www.bbc.co.uk/weather.

4. Compare your chart with the official one.

5. Make amendments to your chart and draw where the fronts should have been.

6. Look at the observations and try to assess why the front is in that position.

With time you will be able to analyse charts more effectively and can even take on the professionals at their own game!

Chart analysis can become addictive, but do be warned: all forecasters analyse charts differently. If I were to give ten professional forecasters exactly the same map for analysis, I would expect ten slightly different charts.

Above all, remember that a chart is there to aid your understanding of the current weather situation. Whilst it is nice for others to see it and understand the weather too, it is primarily *your* chart for *your* purposes.

In the Appendix of this book you will find some charts to practice on.

Here are some of the more commonly used drawings on a chart.

Cloud amounts

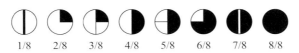

| 1/8 | 2/8 | 3/8 | 4/8 | 5/8 | 6/8 | 7/8 | 8/8 |

Weather

| Mist | Fog | Rain | Drizzle | Snow | Shower | Hail | Thunderstorm |

Basic plotted weather station report

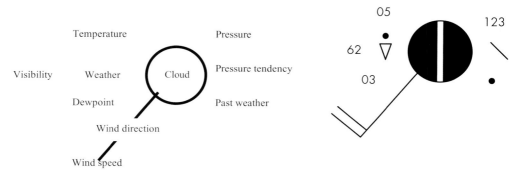

In the report above, the temperature is 5°C and the dew point is 3°C, with 7 oktas of cloud. (Oktas measure the average amount of sky covered by cloud, ranging from 0 oktas for clear skies to 8 oktas for overcast skies.) The wind direction is from the southwest and the wind speed is 20 knots. The visibility was 12 kilometres (62), and the weather reported at the time was a rain shower. The air pressure was 1012.3 millibars, and this was falling. The past weather was rain.

DIY Forecasting from the Charts

Okay, so you have printed out your plotted chart. By now you might even be drawing isobars yourself (easy enough to do every four millibars, but again, practice makes perfect). You will also have plotted fronts, although you may also be looking at an official analysis with the fronts already marked for you.

Note that the chart you are looking at is for a fixed observation time. It is telling you what was happening at the time of the observations, not what is going to happen over the coming hours.

To predict future weather conditions, it is necessary to employ some simple forecasting techniques. Once again, these are easy enough to learn, and regular practice will only improve your technique.

Low Pressure Forecasting

- An area of low pressure will move in the direction of the warm sector (behind the warm front) isobars.

- It will also move towards the region of the greatest falls in pressure (known as the isallobaric low).

- Low pressure will deepen when pressure falls in the warm sector or in the centre of the low itself. (In other words, if a station can be identified as being in the centre of the low, or just past it, but the pressure is still falling, then the low is deepening.)

- Low pressure will fill (i.e., weaken) when pressure rises in the warm sector.

- The low pressure will also fill about 12 to 24 hours after the occluded front starts to form (i.e., when the cold and warm fronts join).

High Pressure Forecasting

Few empirical forecasting rules exist for forecasting high pressure, except for the following:

- High pressure moves towards regions of rising pressure.

- The formation and decay of anticyclones takes longer than depressions.

- Ridges of high pressure build and decay much more rapidly than well-defined areas of high pressure.

Forecasting Wind Speeds

Now that we have a chart, it is a simple matter of using the isobars to estimate wind speeds.

You might think that the only wind speed that can be measured is the surface wind. However, in order to be able to forecast the surface wind, and also predict where a front might be in a few hours' time, we need to be able to make an estimation of the geostrophic wind speed. You are now probably (quite rightly) asking, "What on earth is the geostrophic wind speed?"

Think of the geostrophic wind as the "pure wind". It assumes that the pressure gradient force and Coriolis force are in exact balance and does not take account of the fact that friction reduces the wind speed and backs the wind to the isobars.

By making adjustments to the geostrophic wind speed, one can predict, with some accuracy, wind speed and direction and where fronts might be several hours ahead. Some charts, such as those produced by the UK Meteorological Office, have a geostrophic wind scale printed on them, making it easy to measure the speed (see figure below). On charts which don't have the wind scale marked on them, it is possible to find the speed by using a simple calculation.

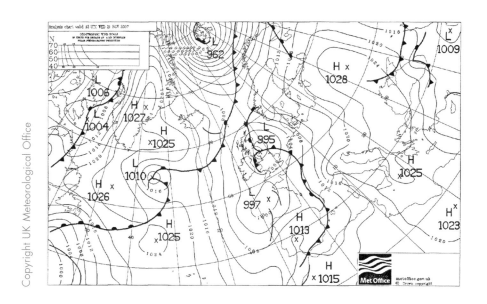

Using the Geostrophic Wind Scale

Some charts include, very helpfully, the geostrophic wind scale. Using these charts it is easy to estimate the wind speed. Let's go through it step by step:

1. Select the area of the country for which you want to measure the geostrophic wind speed. Using a rule or dividers, measure four millibars across the area. Note the latitude of the area (in this case we will assume 52°N).

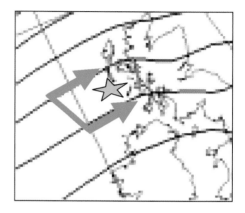

2. The geostrophic wind scale shows latitude down the left-hand side and wind speed top and bottom. Place your rule or dividers against the left of the scale and then measure to the right.

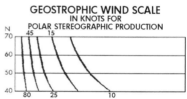

3. Read off the wind speed (you may need to interpolate between two speeds). In this case the wind speed is 18 knots. Well done! Now have a go on your own with other areas of the chart.

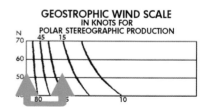

Geostrophic Wind Equation

Most charts do not include a geostrophic wind scale and therefore you have to make the calculations yourself. Don't panic! It is not hard to make the calculation, and with a bit of practice you won't even think about it. A scientific calculator does all the work for you.

Here's how:

1. Measure the distance in nautical miles between two-millibar (2 mb) isobars over the area you wish to calculate the geostrophic wind for (this is "D" in the equation below).

2. Make a note of the latitude of the area you have taken the measurement for (this is "L" in the equation below).

3. Using your measurements for D and L, solve the equation

$$\frac{1176}{D \times \text{sine } L}$$

For example, let's say we are interested in the wind speed over the Isle of Man, and measure 2-mb isobars to be 100 nautical miles (nm) apart at this point (remember that 1 minute of latitude = 1 nm). This gives us D = 100.

The latitude of the Isle of Man is 54°N, therefore L = 54.

Putting this into our equation gives:

$$\frac{1176}{100 \times \text{sine } 54} = \frac{1176}{80.9}$$

The answer is 14.5, so the geostrophic wind speed here is approximately 15 knots.

Estimating the Surface Wind Speed

Once the geostrophic wind speed is found, it is very simple to apply an adjustment to assess the wind speed you are experiencing at the surface.

- Over the sea the surface wind is approximately 66% (two thirds) of the geostrophic wind.

- Over land the surface wind is approximately 33% (one third) of the geostrophic wind.

The above is only a rule of thumb and some adjustments do need to be made. For example, if the isobars show a lot of curvature, then the speed should be reduced.

Gusts are not accounted for in the above, either. As a rough rule of thumb, the gusts over the sea will tend to be around 1.3 times the mean hourly wind speed. Over land, especially in cities, this gust factor can increase to as much as twice the hourly wind speed.

REMEMBER

Actual wind speeds are

66%	**33%**
of the geostrophic speed	*of the geostrophic speed*
over the sea	**over the land**

Forecasting the Movements of Fronts

If you are able to measure the speed of the geostrophic wind, then you will also be able to predict the movements of fronts on a weather map.

The method for doing this is to measure the distance between two isobars *along* the front. Measuring from the left of the geostrophic wind scale, or using the geostrophic wind equation, assess the speed of the geostrophic wind.

Next, use the following rules to determine the speed of movements of the fronts on your chart:

- **Warm fronts** move at about two thirds the speed of the geostrophic wind

- **Cold fronts** move at about the geostrophic wind speed

- **Occluded fronts** move at about the geostrophic wind speed

- **Troughs** move at about the geostrophic wind speed.

Calculations can then be made to estimate how far the front will move.

Example: Calculating the Movement of a Warm Front

If the geostrophic wind across a warm front is 20 knots, how far will the front move in six hours? Recall that a warm front moves at two thirds the speed of the geostrophic wind, thus

$$\left(\frac{20\times6}{3}\right)\times 2 = 80\,\text{nm}$$

The front will move 80 nautical miles in six hours.

If the geostrophic speed along a cold front is measured at 30 knots, the front will move 180 nm in six hours, that is, 30 × 6 = 180 nm. (Recall that cold fronts move at the geostrophic speed.)

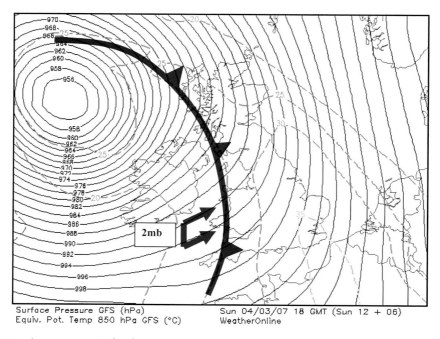

Surface Pressure GFS (hPa)   Sun 04/03/07 18 GMT (Sun 12 + 06)
Equiv. Pot. Temp 850 hPa GFS (°C)   WeatherOnline

Predicting the movement of a front

Example: Calculating the Movement of a Cold Front

How far will the cold front in the chart move after six hours? In this example, the geostrophic wind speed is not given on the chart and must be calculated.

1. Measure the distance between the 2-mb isobars (remember 1 minute = 1 nm). In this case the distance D is ~70 nm. The latitude (L) is 52°N.

2. Plugging into the geostrophic wind equation gives

$$\frac{1176}{70 \times \text{sine } 52} = \frac{1176}{78.8} = 14.9$$

3. This gives an answer of about 15 knots.

4. Recall that cold fronts move at geostrophic speed. So, if the front is moving at 15 knots, in three hours it will have moved $15 \times 3 = 45$ nm.

Observing the Weather

You cannot understand the weather until you can observe accurately and competently. Taking a regular observation of the weather, whether you have instruments on-board or are simply using your eyes, enables you to learn how weather develops over time.

The first thing to do is to make a journal. This could be a small diary or a plain book. I recommend that you make a note of where you are, the weather event that is occurring and any other information that is to hand.

In time you will see how weather develops and will be able to spot fronts moving in. For example, spotting the first cirrus clouds, watching them lowering to altostratus and eventually nimbostratus and rain, then seeing visibility reduce and temperatures rise.

So what if you can't identify the clouds, or you don't have access to a thermometer? You can still note what the weather feels like and then over time you

One cannot observe the weather until accurate observations can be made.

can add more information as you become more competent. Why not make a resolution to yourself today that you will start a weather notebook?

If you do have access to instruments, make a note of the readings they give, together with your own observations. The most useful instruments on-board, at least as far as I am concerned, are the barometer and barograph. Amongst other things these can help you forecast how quickly the weather is improving, or deteriorating. A thermometer is useful too, as is some method for accurately measuring the wind.

Self-teaching in weather is the key to success and I still keep a daily weather journal. Yes, there are other things in one's life to be doing, but it doesn't take much time for this to become a habit, and a quick note of the weather takes seconds to write down.

Forecasting from the Clouds

They float majestically above our heads, but clouds can give the sailor plenty of information about the weather, including that which is likely to occur over the coming hours.

Some of the names of clouds may be familiar to you: cumulus, cirrus, cumulonimbus. This nomenclature was first suggested by a young chemist called Luke Howard at a lecture entitled "On the Modification of Clouds", in 1802. The story of how Howard named clouds is a fascinating one and is wonderfully described in a book by Richard Hamblyn entitled *The Invention of Clouds*.

Today we use many of the same names, with minor changes, as those suggested by Howard. Over the following pages we consider how clouds affect the weather and can help the sailor predict future conditions.

We can break down clouds into three main categories; high, medium and low:

- High clouds: above 18,000 ft

- Medium clouds: 6000 to 18,000 ft

- Low clouds: below 6000 ft

Clouds have been assigned official designations depending upon the height at which their bases occur:

- High clouds: cirrus, cirrostratus, cirrocumulus
- Medium clouds: altocumulus, altostratus, nimbostratus
- Low clouds: stratus, cumulus, stratocumulus, cumulonimbus

Nimbostratus is a strange cloud in that it falls between low and medium level clouds, as its base can occur at either of these levels. Whether its base is low or medium, however, nimbostratus always brings rain.

Let's now look at each of the clouds mentioned above.

High Clouds: Cirrus

Cirrus clouds, sometimes known as mare's tales, are the familiar high, wispy clouds we see on a fine summer day. They are easy to identify and occur mainly above 20,000 ft. Cirrus clouds are useful in identifying how mobile the weather situation is and are usually the first sign that a warm front is on its way.

Cirrus Indicating a Mobile, Changeable Situation

If the cirrus clouds are in long streaks, it may indicate a jet stream, in which case the weather is very mobile and likely to change. Should cirrus increase and thicken into cirrostratus, one might expect rain within 7 to 10 hours.

Cirrus Indicating Showers and Troughs

If cirrus is a long way in the distance, perhaps just on the horizon, watch carefully. It may be that you are seeing the top of a large cumulonimbus cloud, which could mean that a trough or thunderstorm is on the way (this is more relevant in the tropics).

Cirrus Indicating Little Change and Fine Weather

If cirrus is in thin wisps and alters little over a couple of hours, changes in the weather are likely to be slow, and fine weather will probably persist. Watch the barometer for falling pressure to indicate that the weather may be changing.

High Clouds: Cirrostratus

Cirrostratus clouds are similar to dense cirrus clouds, and often thicken into a veil of white cloud. They can cause a halo to form around the sun or moon and occur above 18,000 ft. If cirrostratus thickens from cirrus, this is a good indicator that a warm front is on the way. The cloud can also mark an improvement as a front clears.

Cirrostratus Indicating a Deterioration

If the cloud thickens from cirrus into cirrostratus, then you should be thinking "Aha, warm front!" Should a halo form around the sun or moon, rain is usually around 4 to 8 hours away. You will know which direction the rain is coming from, as this is the direction from which the halo breaks first. Watch the barometer carefully; if it is falling, then the picture of a deterioration should be clear in your mind. Should the barometer be falling quickly (more than two millibars in an hour), then the winds are likely to become very strong.

Cirrostratus Indicating an Improvement

If the cirrostratus is following rain and cloud begins to break showing the cloud, this usually indicates that the improvement will continue. Check the barometer. If it is rising, this should confirm that conditions will get better over the coming hours.

High Clouds: Cirrocumulus

Cirrocumulus clouds are very high clouds that appear as small cumulus-type masses. They indicate instability at upper levels in the atmosphere and can be easily confused with altocumulus clouds. They can occur anywhere above 18,000 ft and are a fairly elusive cloud.

Cirrocumulus Indicating a Deterioration

There are a few indicators to watch for in cirrocumulus clouds. The main aspect of a deterioration is an influx of more unstable air at upper levels. If you start to see altocumulus castellanus clouds (see later), then this could confirm that a destabilisation is taking place and that showers may occur, or even thunderstorms in summer months.

Medium Clouds: Altocumulus

Altocumulus clouds can appear as one of the most dramatic in the sky. As in the picture they can often look like fish-scales, which has led to them being referred to as a "mackerel sky". They appear between 6,000 and 18,000 ft, and if they follow cirrus and cirrostratus can indicate that a warm front is on the way, especially if they then blend into altostratus. If the clouds appear more bubble-like, they can indicate thunderstorms.

Altocumulus Indicating a Deterioration

If the clouds appear after cirrus and cirrostratus, this can mean that rain is on the way, perhaps within two to three hours, associated with a warm front.

Altocumulus Indicating Thunderstorms

Appearing like castle turrets in the sky, these clouds are known as altocumulus castellanus. They show deep instability through the atmosphere, especially if cumulus are in evidence too, and show that heavy showers or thunderstorms can be expected.

Altocumulus Indicating Fair Weather

If the clouds are in patches and do not evolve much, the weather is unlikely to change. However, do remember that by their nature altocumulus show that unstable air is aloft.

Medium Clouds: Altostratus

As grey, uniform clouds, altostratus often appear as a featureless layer. The sun or moon may slowly disappear behind them, possibly causing halos. They usually occur between 6,000 and 18,000 ft and ahead of warm fronts and are the first rain-bearing clouds of the frontal system.

Altostratus Ahead of the Warm Front

If altostratus has thickened over the preceding hours from cirrus, cirrostratus and altocumulus, we can be fairly sure that the warm front is almost upon us. A glance at the falling barometer will confirm this.

At the first appearance of the altostratus halo, rain can usually be expected within the hour. Once the halo disappears, rain is imminent and the sailor should be prepared for increasing winds and falling visibility as the rain becomes more persistent.

Remember that all the timings shown in this section on clouds are approximate and apply to the "average" weather system. Used with the barometer or barograph the sailor can get a good indication as to how fast a weather system is approaching.

Medium Clouds: Nimbostratus

Nimbostratus clouds are rain-bearing clouds. The bases of them can occur anywhere between 100 and 7000 ft and are often ragged. These are the clouds which produce dark days and continuous rain for several hours.

Nimbostratus Weather Indicators

If the bases of the clouds are ragged, it is probably already raining where you are. If nimbostratus is overhead, then you are very close to the warm front. Rain is probably going to be moderate, and the barometer will still be falling. Winds will be gusty and visibility will be deteriorating.

Watch for signs of the sky brightening and the barometer becoming more steady. The wind will also veer, indicating that the warm front has passed through. Rain will be turning to drizzle and visibility will further deteriorate. If this is the case, then you should watch carefully for signs of a cold front approaching: the barometer will fall, winds increase and it will start raining again.

Low Clouds: Stratus

A grey, indistinguishable cloud, stratus often occurs behind the warm front. It can also occur inland on still, winter days, under high pressure. Stratus can produce drizzle and its base can be anywhere from the surface to about 1200 ft.

Stratus Weather Indicators

Stratus cloud does not have enough vertical extent to produce rain, but it can produce drizzle. If it is raining underneath stratus, this means there must be another layer of cloud above from which the rain is falling through the stratus cloud.

It is stratus clouds which produce the drizzle in the warm sector of the frontal system. If the cloud is fractured below its base, it can be a sign that rain is not far away.

Low Clouds: Stratocumulus

Stratocumulus clouds (you may hear a forecaster refer to them as "strato-cu") are the most common clouds experienced in the UK and Ireland. Almost not a day passes without a weather station reporting seeing these clouds. Stratocumulus is indicative of a stable atmosphere. It is a "rolling" cloud, and these rolls can often be seen where air has risen, cooled and condensed and then sunk again back to its original level (described in Chapter 1). The cloud usually occurs between about 1500 ft and 6000 ft.

Stratocumulus Weather Indicators

Being a shallow cloud, any rain that falls from stratocumulus is only light. Should moderate or heavy rain be falling from stratocumulus, it will be cloud above which is actually producing this.

As a stable cloud, stratocumulus tends to indicate no great changes in the weather over the coming hours, and you will probably notice the barometer remaining fairly steady during this time.

Low Clouds: Cumulus

Cumulus clouds are the cotton-wool clouds we see so frequently on a summer day, although they may occur at any time of the year. If cumulus do occur, it's important to watch them for a few hours to see whether they grow. Forming by convection, they may develop into thunderclouds. Occurring between about 1200 and 6000 ft, they give a lot of information about the upper atmosphere.

Cumulus Indicating Fine Weather

Always watch cumulus carefully through the day. If they form but change little from morning to afternoon, this is a good indication that the weather will stay fair.

Cumulus Indicating Showers

If the cumulus grow suddenly, either from small morning cumulus or during the heat of the afternoon, watch for darkening bases; this may mean showers are imminent. If they grow further, then this could indicate thunderstorms are on their way.

Cumulus Indicating the Onset of a Warm Front

If cumulus are present, and then cirrus appear above them, they may start to lose their vertical extent. Check the barometer. If it's falling, a warm front could be on the way.

Low Clouds: Cumulonimbus

Probably the most famous of all clouds, the mighty cumulonimbus is the classic thundercloud. A large convective cloud, it may have an anvil-shaped top and can occur anywhere from 200 to 6,000 ft, although I have seen them reported as high as 8,000 ft. They indicate a deeply unstable atmosphere and can lead to heavy showers, hail, thunderstorms, gale force gusts, tornadoes and even waterspouts.

Cumulonimbus Weather Indicators

In the next chapter there is a section about thunderstorms detailing how cumulonimbus clouds form, why and when. The best advice I can give is to avoid them if you can!

Cumulonimbus clouds generate their own environment and may be referred to as "super-cells". If enough surface observations are available, it is sometimes possible to clearly identify warm, cold and occluded fronts underneath the clouds.

If you are in an air mass in which cumulonimbus are occurring, watch the barometer or barograph, as this will give you most information about whether a storm cloud is approaching or retreating from you.

The Whisper of the Winds

Predicting the winds local to one's sailing area not only can enhance your sailing, but may also add to the comfort of passengers and crew.

The winds I will cover, and which are most important to the sailor, are:

- Sea and land breezes

- Katabatic and anabatic winds

- Acceleration zones

- Convergence zones

A katabatic wind flows down the valley sides, creating a pool of cold air.

Models may sometimes be able to predict these or give a general indication as to the likelihood of their onset and magnitude; more often than not, though, it's down to the sailor to predict the likelihood of them occurring.

Sea Breezes

These are breezes which are caused by an imbalance of heating between the land and the sea. Remember we said that the air always tried to achieve balance? Well, if you remove air from one section of the atmosphere, air from elsewhere will rush in to replace it, and that is the principle of sea and land breezes.

A sea breeze is simply a local circulation caused by convection. Warm air rises over the land, reduces pressure and makes air flow from higher pressure over the sea to fill the hole left by the rising air over land (our fourth principle of the weather).

Sea breezes are best viewed in pictures, so let's start with the situation at 8 a.m. on a late May morning.

1. Skies are clear, with a light offshore breeze. The sea and land temperatures are the same at 18°C. Winds are light and the air is in balance.

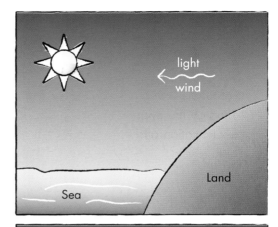

2. By 10 a.m. the sun has heated the land to 15°C, whilst the sea stays at 10°C. As the warm air rises over the land, pressure falls, creating a hole. Pressure is now higher over the sea than over land, and the air flows from high to low pressure.

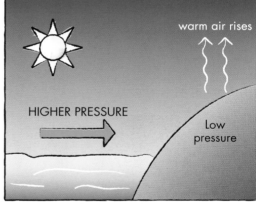

3. By midday the sea temperature has risen to 11°C, with the air temperature at 20°C. As the more dense air moves inland, it undercuts the warm air, already rising. The offshore flow then pushes the wind offshore at higher levels. This then cools, sinks, and completes the circulation.

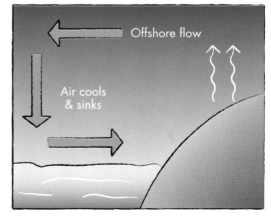

It is important to note that a calm zone is created by the sea breeze offshore in the zone where the air sinks. This zone will tend to move out to sea during the course of the afternoon as the sea breeze strengthens.

Winds directions will veer as the breeze strengthens and generally settles to be at around 20 degrees to the shoreline.

Through the evening the offshore flow will begin again and "blow" the sea breeze circulation offshore, before it finally blows out overnight.

Sea breezes in the UK occur from March to late September, with most between May and August. They generally begin to move inland around 11 a.m. and can extend inland by more than 50 nautical miles by 11 p.m.

Sea breeze front

You may have noticed that in (3) above the dense cold air undercuts the less dense warm air as it moves inland. It may have occurred to you that this is similar to a cold front. Indeed, this change in air mass (from a mini-continental flow to a mini-maritime flow) is known as a sea breeze front.

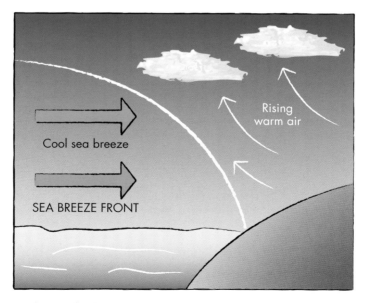

Diagram of a sea breeze front

The sea breeze front marks a sharp transition zone between the cool sea air and the warm land air. At this point air is forced to rise, cool and condense, with cumuliform clouds forming along the zone of this rising air.

Cumulus clouds can often be large, and showers do occur along this front. It is also possible to have thunderstorms associated with the front as it moves inland to ever hotter conditions.

From the sea, sailors can often witness the sea breeze front as it moves inland, especially along English Channel coasts. The sea breeze front is of more significance, at least weatherwise, to those inland; but remember that as the front moves further inland, the calm zone of the sea breeze will be moving closer to shore.

Land Breezes

The land breeze is essentially the phenomenon opposite to the sea breeze. It occurs when the temperature of the sea is warmer than the land. The rising motion of the air over the sea results in lower pressure and air draining off the land to fill the hole left by the rising air.

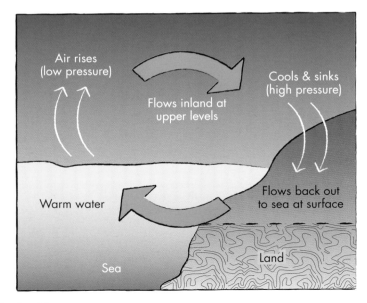

Diagram of a land breeze

Experience shows that the land breeze is rarely as well defined as the sea breeze. However, be aware of them. On a night (particularly in late summer) when temperatures inland are forecast to fall sharply, a breeze may be created close to the shore when out at sea the wind may be calm.

Katabatic Wind

The katabatic wind is caused by dense, cool air flowing down a slope. They are felt by the sailor as a strong wind flowing from the shore, and will feel cold. Here's how they form:

1. Imagine a valley. As the sun sets, the air on top of the hills cools quicker than the air in the valley. The cooler air is more dense and so flows down the valley slopes, displacing and cooling the warmer air in the bottom of the valley.

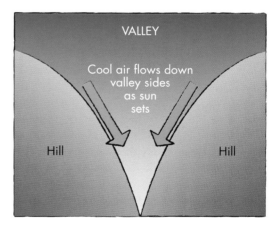

2. If the valley is well aligned, then the air will flow out to sea, as a cold wind. A river estuary with steep sides, or even large sand dunes, could be sufficient to produce a katabatic wind.

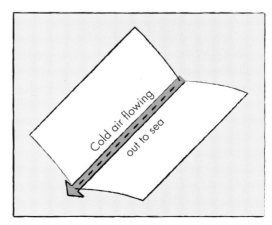

It is also worth remembering that with a "cold pool" of air in the bottom of the valley, fog may more readily form here and perhaps be blown towards the coasts and out to sea.

Anabatic Wind

The anabatic wind is essentially the opposite to the katabatic wind and occurs during the mornings.

1. As the sun rises during the morning, the tops of valley hills are heated more quickly than the valley floor (where there may be mist and fog due to the cold drainage from the previous night).

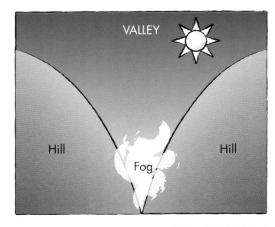

2. The heated air at the tops of the valley rises, and lowers pressure here. This causes the air at the valley bottom (under high pressure) to flow upslope toward the valley tops and the air to flow from the sea inland.

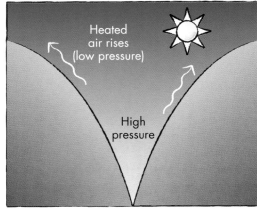

It is easy for a sailor to mistake an anabatic wind for the onset of a sea breeze. Look at the shape and contours of the land if you are in unfamiliar waters and assess whether an anabatic wind is possible.

Acceleration Zones and Rotor Waves

The sailor should always be aware of the possibility of sailing in acceleration zones and of rotor waves. These are created by, and occur around, mountainous island groups such as the Canary Islands and the Greek islands.

Acceleration zones can increase winds speeds by up to 3 Beaufort forces and are often not highlighted by local forecasts. Rotor waves can generate strong gusts to the leeward side of the mountains.

Rotor Waves

Rotor waves form as shown in the following diagrams.

Lenticularis cloud often signify the presence of rotor waves.

1. Winds flow towards a mountainous island. The air can either travel around the island or over the top of it. Some air is therefore forced to rise.

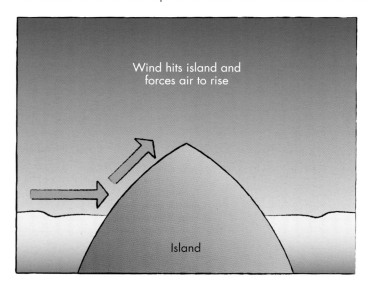

2. If the air hits a warmer layer above the islands, this may prevent further ascent. The air is deflected back down the mountain (to the leeward side). In effect the air "tumbles" down the mountain and can form very gusty winds.

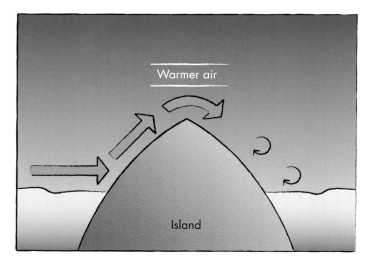

Prediction of acceleration zones by the sailor is actually quite straightforward. First, if you are going to be sailing around island groups, you should always be aware of the possibility of increased winds.

Second, look at the wind direction. If it is aligned with the gaps between the islands, then chances of enhanced winds are increased.

Third, if warm air is aloft, for example, after the passage of a warm front, this can enhance the possibility of an acceleration zone forming.

Rotor waves are more difficult to predict. However, one can watch for a "rotor cloud" capping the mountain top. Seas may also be choppy on the leeward side of the mountain and this should be seen by the sailor.

Convergence Zones

A convergence zone occurs where air is traveling at different speeds or in differing directions.

The main examples affecting the sailor typically occur because of a disparity in wind speed and direction between the land and the sea.

We have already seen that the wind travels faster over the sea than over the land due to friction being much less over the smoother sea surface. This causes air coming off the sea to "pile up" as it hits and slows down overland. Normally, this does not have too much of a noticeable effect on the weather, but if the atmosphere is finely poised, the forced rising of the air could be enough to trigger showers.

Hazards

Thunderstorms

Mist and Fog

Thunderstorms

Apart from the threat posed by strong winds and rough seas, day-to-day sailors face most hazards brought about by thunderstorms and fog.

An understanding of how and why these phenomena occur can certainly help in their prediction.

Three key ingredients are needed to generate a thunderstorm. These are:

- An unstable atmosphere

- A moist atmosphere

- A mechanism to force ascent, such as heating (thermals), hills and mountains or a frontal slope.

Once these factors are in place, the chance of a thunderstorm developing is increased.

However, as we all know only too well, there are days when thunderstorms are forecast and all that is seen throughout the day is a small, white, fluffy cumulus cloud. These events often occur because one of the other ingredients weren't quite in place. For example, it may be that there wasn't enough moisture available in the atmosphere for a thunderstorm to form.

Thunderstorm hazards include gusty winds, hail, lightning and icing (in the winter). The best thing to do is to avoid severe storms if you can (easier said than done!).

A Day in the Life of a Thunderstorm

1. Early stage: moist air rises and is cooled to its dew point. Latent heat is released, aiding the rising air. Pressure falls and air from lower levels is "sucked in" to replace that which has risen. Small to moderate cumulus clouds form.

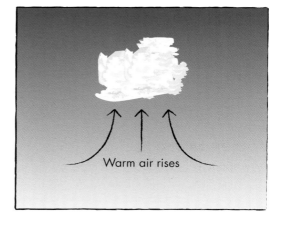
Warm air rises

2. Mature stage: water vapour condenses into large droplets. These fall through the cloud creating downdrafts. Droplets could be forced to rise again, possibly forming hail. The thunderstorm is triggered and at this stage the storm is extremely hazardous. Downbursts may cause very gusty winds on reaching the surface, known as a gust front.

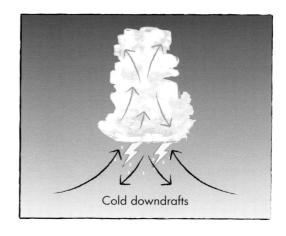
Cold downdrafts

3. Dissipating stage: the storm is now old and losing its energy. This normally occurs at the end of the day when heat energy is lost. Only cold downdrafts are left and no more vertical development is taking pace. Precipitation ceases and the cloud will eventually collapse and disperse.

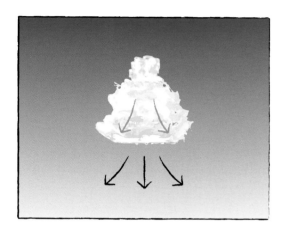

Mist and Fog

For a given temperature the atmosphere will hold only a limited amount of water as vapour.

If the air mass is sufficiently moist, once a particular temperature is reached, the vapour will condense out into minute, visible droplets; mist and fog will form.

Types of Fog

There are three types of fog:

- Radiation fog, which forms because of the reduction of temperature, usually inland on a clear, cool night

- Advection fog, caused by warmer or cold temperatures moving in (advecting) from elsewhere

- Hill fog, which is cloud covering the hilltops

Radiation Fog

Usually forming on a clear night with light winds, radiation fog occurs inland. It isn't a major problem for coastal sailors, but can be blown towards the coasts.

Radiation fog forms on cool, clear nights.

For radiation fog to form, certain circumstances are required:

- Clear skies

- Moist air

- Falling temperatures, close to the dew point

- Light winds (5 to 7 knots), which mix air in the lower levels aiding the fog formation

It is possible to forecast the formation of radiation fog. As with all things "forecasting", it is necessary to keep a watchful eye on weather conditions and spot the circumstances for its development. The sailor should look at the forecast charts for midnight and 6 A.M. and then ask a series of questions:

- Is there a ridge of high pressure over the area of interest, or a col?

- Will skies be clear?

- What will wind speeds be? (5 to 7 knots?)

- Will dew points fall, rise or stay the same? Dew points do not vary as much through the day as do temperatures. Monitor the afternoon dew points.

- Will wind speeds increase or decrease overnight to fall within the ideal 5- to 7-knot range?

- Will cloud increase or decrease overnight? If cloud increases, temperatures will increase; if cloud decreases, temperatures will fall.

If you're wondering how to predict temperature and dew points, several Web sites (such as Weatheronline) now offer forecasts of dew points and temperatures throughout the night.

Advection (Coastal Fog)

This is the fog that affects sailors most often. The classic advection fog occurs on western and southern coasts of the British Isles and Ireland.

As its name suggests, advection fog is fog caused by warmer air being advected in from another location.

Typical locations in the UK and Ireland for advection and coastal fog are southwest England, Wales, southern and western Ireland, northwest England and the west coasts of Scotland.

Advection fog forms in the following way:

- A moist flow of air is present, usually in a tropical maritime air mass

- Moist warm air flows over a colder sea (e.g., warm air from the Azores traveling over cooler Atlantic waters southwest of the UK)

- Warmer air contains more moisture than cold air, and so as the warm air comes into contact with a colder sea, it can no longer hold the water as invisible vapour

- The water vapour condenses and forms fog

The most common fog to sailors is advection fog.

A classic scenario is for advection fog to form in the warm sector, behind a warm front.

Note that unlike radiation fog, wind speed is not a factor in the formation of advection fog.

A similar effect occurs when cold air flows over a warm sea. The air in contact with the sea can no longer hold its water as invisible vapour and so condenses. This phenomena is often seen in the Arctic and is referred to as Arctic sea smoke.

To forecast advection fog, you should ask yourself:

- How moist is the air?

- What are the dew points downwind? Are they higher or lower than the current dew points?

- Is the sea cold or warm when compared with the air mass above it?

- Where did the air mass originate?

Advection fog is well forecast in the Shipping and Inshore Waters Forecasts, so you should be alerted to the possibility of it occurring. However, it's always useful to be able to spot the circumstances leading to advection fog formation, as a slight change in wind direction could mean the difference between good and poor visibility.

Where to Get Weather Information

The Shipping Forecast

One of the most well known and greatest of British institutions is the Shipping Forecast. Its melodic tones provide comfort to sailors and to those who are on-shore, safely tucked up in their beds.

Issued four times daily, the Shipping Forecast provides forecasts of offshore weather conditions around the coasts of the UK and western Europe. For those sailors closer to shore (within 12 miles), the Inshore Waters Forecasts, issued twice daily, provide a detailed overview of conditions expected over the following 24 hours.

Shipping Forecasts can be viewed online at various Web sites, including my own at http://www.weatherweb.net/uksail.htm and the Meteorological Office at http://meto.gov.uk. Of course, the more usual way to receive the forecasts is to listen to them on BBC Radio 4. Daily broadcast times are as follows:

Longwave (198 kHz) and FM (various frequencies) at 0048 and 0520

Longwave only (198 kHz) at 1200 and 1755

Inshore Waters Forecasts are heard on BBC Radio 4 and BBC Radio 3 as follows:

Longwave (198 kHz) at 0048 (after the Shipping Forecasts)

Radio 3, FM only (various frequencies) at 0535

As well as forecasts, actual weather reports for weather stations around the UK and Ireland coasts are broadcast with the 0048 and 0535 bulletins. These consist of reports of wind direction and speed, visibility, weather, pressure and pressure tendency.

I now want to take a look at the Shipping Forecast in more detail. Of course, the best way to learn is to familiarise yourself with the forecasts by listening to them. Technology has made this easier by using listening on demand. Just visit the Radio 4 homepage at http://www.bbc.co.uk/radio4 and click on the "Shipping Forecast" button to hear the latest forecast.

The Shipping Forecast

Shipping Forecast Areas

The familiar names we hear on the Shipping Forecast correspond to a specific area. Names have been given largely because of specific features within that area, for example, Dogger Bank, although one of the newest names, "FitzRoy", is named after the first Director General of the Meteorological Office.

Starting with Viking and following roughly clockwise around the map, the area forecasts are always read in the same order. If the forecast is the same for several consecutive areas, these will be amalgamated, with the area names read together. The forecast is then given for those areas.

The order of forecasts is always: Viking, North Utsire, South Utsire, Forties, Cromarty, Forth, Tyne, Dogger, Fisher, German Bight, Humber, Thames, Dover, Wight, Portland, Plymouth, Biscay, Trafalgar (0048 bulletin only), FitzRoy, Sole, Lundy, Fastnet, Irish Sea, Shannon, Rockall, Malin, Hebrides, Bailey, Fair Isle, Faeroes and Southeast Iceland.

Now, here's an admission. My party piece is being able to recite all the Shipping Forecast area names in the correct order within 1 minute (yes, I know!). My passion for weather grew when, from the age of 13, for many years I loyally recorded and transcribed every Shipping Forecast. As you can tell, I wasn't your average teenager!

Shipping Forecast Broadcast Order

Each forecast always follows the same order, which is:

1. An introduction stating the time and date that the forecast was issued. For example: *"Here is the Shipping Forecast issued by the Met Office on behalf of the Maritime and Coastguard Agency at 1105 BST today, Wednesday 1st August 2007."*

2. Gale warnings: If winds are expected to exceed Beaufort force 8 in any area, that area is named. Should there not be any gales forecast, this section will be omitted. For example, *"There are warnings of gales in Viking, Wight and Biscay."*

Each forecast always begins with Cape Wrath, then moves clockwise around the coasts of the United Kingdom and eastern Northern Ireland.

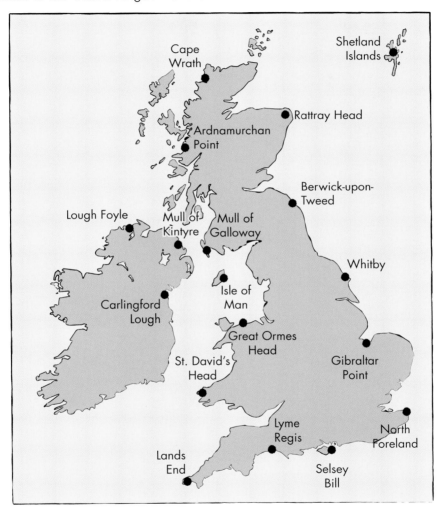

Inshore Waters Broadcast Order

As with the Shipping Forecast, each forecast follows the same order, which is:

1. An introduction stating the time and date that the forecast was issued. For example, "*Here is the weather forecast for the inshore waters of*

Great Britain and Northern Ireland issued by the Met Office at 0530 GMT on Wednesday 1st August 2007 and valid for the following 18 hours."

2. General Synopsis: Giving a detailed statement of the position of fronts and pressure systems which directly affect the British Isles and an indication as to their likely movement. For example, "And now the General Synopsis at 0700. Low pressure will move slowly northeastwards, just east of Iceland, with associated weakening rain band moving southeast over the British Isles."

3. Area Forecasts: A forecast is then given for each area, with details of wind direction, strength, weather and visibility, together with any changes that are expected. For example, "From Cape Wrath to Duncansby Head including Orkney. West or southwest 5 to 7. Showers. Visibility, good."

A Great British Institution

The Shipping and Inshore Waters Forecasts are probably the best forecasts available freely to the public in the British Isles. In fact, they may be considered amongst the best forecasts issued anywhere in the word.

Being written by experienced meteorologists, not by computer, the forecasts are written with mariners in mind. Of course, there are occasions when the forecasts may be wrong, but their accuracy is closely monitored.

If you get conflicting forecasts from a computer-generated forecast compared with the human-produced Shipping and Inshore Waters Forecasts, always lean towards the latter. The expert forecaster will probably have looked at the same information as you and will have decided against using some of the data in his or her forecast.

If you are at sea, keep a close eye on conditions. If they appear to be developing against the predictions given in the Shipping or Inshore Waters forecast, ask yourself, "Why should this be?" Some of the questions that may spring to mind include: Has a sea breeze developed? Has a low pressure area deepened more rapidly than expected? Has the movement of a front slowed down (or speeded up)? The reason for the change should become clear when the next forecast is issued.

I would urge all mariners to use the Shipping and Inshore Waters Forecast. They should become familiar with them, and trust them. They are a great British institution and long may they reign.

Internet Weather Charts

How things have changed in the last ten years! When I first started weather forecasting in the mid-1980s, the height of forecasting technology for the amateur was a shortwave radio, a fax decoder and a dot-matrix printer. The latter two printed weather charts and coded weather reports for plotting and decoding. One hoped that the radio signal would not fade before the chart was completed, and sod's law was usually that the radio signal faded just as your area was being printed on the map. The result was a black smudge through the chart!

Of course, radiofax is still very much alive and is a vital addition to a vessel's weather arsenal, especially if you are planning lengthier passages such as a cross-Channel trip or a tour of the Atlantic Islands.

Most sailors in-port, though, will nowadays have access to a computer. Indeed, many sailors will also now have high-speed Internet access within a few miles offshore. This allows for a bewildering amount of weather charts to be shown to the sailor from thousands of sources. Of course, the question is, which Internet sites and which charts to use and trust?

This section is intended to help you by introducing sites that I hope you will be interested in. It may be that you have seen these before, although background information about the sites may be useful.

Weatheronline.co.uk (http://www.weatheronline.co.uk)

A German-owned weather company (wetteronline.de), Weatheronline.co.uk provides some of the best weather information on the web for sailors.

Navigation can sometimes be not particularly easy as there is so much data available on the site.

Raw weather charts from various models are available under the "Expert Weather" section from the homepage. Here you can see charts out to 384 hours (from the GFS model), updated four times daily, as well as the UK Met Office and

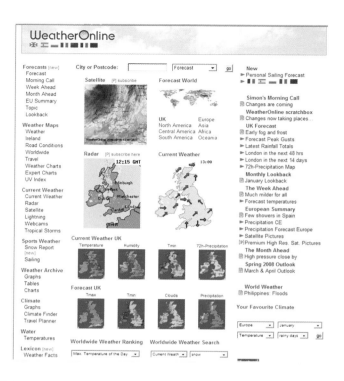

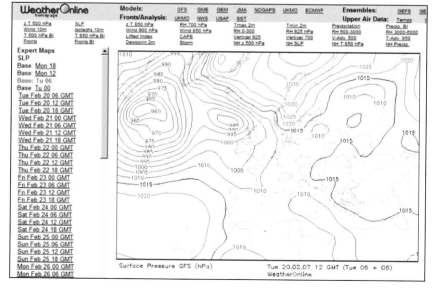

GFS ensemble models. These charts do need some interpretation, but as with so much in weather forecasting, if you can familiarise yourself with the charts, you will soon get used to using them and will have a deeper understanding of the forecast.

Some sailing forecasts are provided too. From the home page scroll down to "Sports Weather" and click on "Sailing". You will be taken to a page with a map of the Mediterranean. Across the top of the page are geographical regions to select, so by clicking on "Great Britain" you can select three-hour wind forecasts for the British Isles and Ireland out to several days ahead.

By clicking further into a region you can get reports giving forecasts of wind speeds (and gusts) in a text format. Coastal station reports, tide information and satellite images are also available from the site. You can also access the site via your mobile telephone.

Wetterzentrale.de (http://www.wetterzentrale.de)

This is another German-run Web site, and one that has been established longest. On reaching the home page, click on the "Top Karten" link. This takes you to the page that lists all of the model forecasts available on this site.

In the top left-hand corner you will see various options listed. These include being able to see satellite and radar pictures, but also links to various models, including the GFS, UK Met Office, Canadian weather service and many more.

The charts extend as far ahead as 384 hours, and again getting used to the presentation and format of the charts will enable the sailor to become adept at using them for forecasting purposes.

The final option on the models menu is "Wellen/Wind". This is a rather coarse, colour-coded representation of forecast wind speed and direction out to 126 hours for any location in the world.

Something which I find of particular interest on the site is the list of archived charts that are available. These give the familiar fax analysis charts back to 1998, ideal for checking up on the weather when you have one of those "remember that gale in 1991" moments.

Other archived charts include reanalysis charts dating back to 1880. These are ideal for checking what the weather chart looked like for D-Day or for looking at the weather station for the disastrous Fastnet race of 1979.

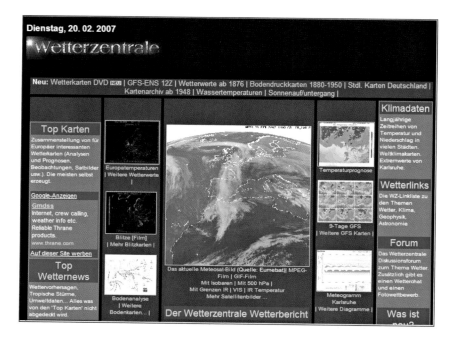

Init : Fri,28DEC2007 12Z   Valid: Sat,29DEC2007 00Z
500 hPa Geopot.(gpdm), T (C) und Bodendr. (hPa)

Daten: GFS—Modell des amerikanischen Wetterdienstes
(C) Wetterzentrale
www.wetterzentrale.de

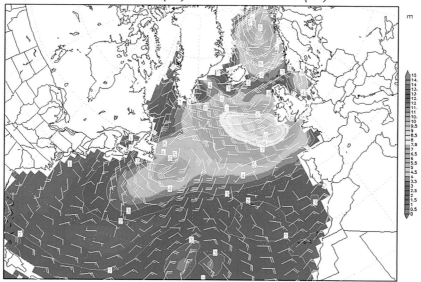

Init : Fri,28DEC2007 06Z   Valid: Sat,29DEC2007 00Z
Wellenhoehe (m) und 10m Wind (kt)

Westwind (http://www.westwind.ch)

Unlike the other Web sites mentioned here, the Switzerland-based Westwind site does not produce its own charts or forecasts. Instead, it collects links to many different forecasting models and sites and lists them on one easy-to-use page. I use

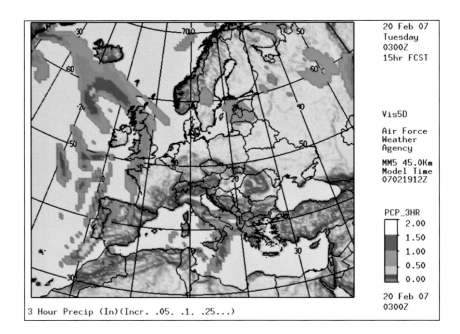

Westwind several times a day to check the latest model output, as it has proved very reliable over the years and is easier than having lists of one's own links. As well as model-based forecasts, you can also link through to current weather observations, satellite, radar and lightning strike pictures.

For sailors there is a link to "Sea Models". Clicking on this will allow another drop-down menu box to appear. This lists various models which make predictions of wind, sea state, wave direction and wave periods.

All in all, Westwind is a one-stop-shop site; not only is there a variety of model-based forecasts, but it also provides useful information about current weather conditions.

This is another site which is well worth spending a few hours having a look around. You never know what you will find.

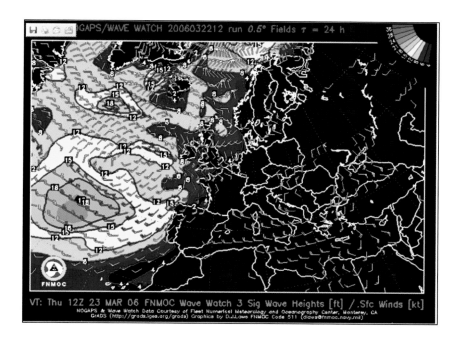

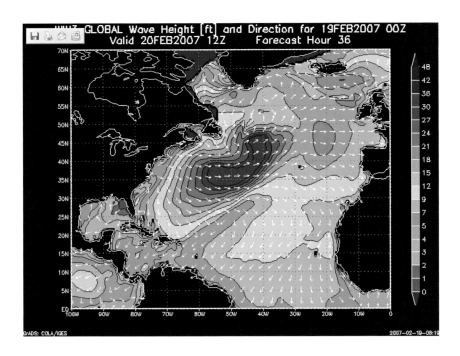

National Buoy Data Center (http://www.ndbc.noaa.gov)

This excellent site is provided by the United States National Weather Service. It contains links to weather observations made by automatic buoys located at various locations around the world.

The buoys are provided by national weather services and private concerns, such as oil companies. Data are made freely available in order to enhance the quality of forecasting and to improve the safety of life at sea.

The home page highlights areas where the data are available. Click on one of the grey boxes and this will zoom in to a map of the area you are interested in. Each of the buoys is then listed on the map. Select one of these and you will see the latest weather report from this buoy, a log of conditions during the preceding 24 hours and sometimes even a picture of the buoy. Observational data include wind speed and direction, wind gusts, wave height and period, air pressure,

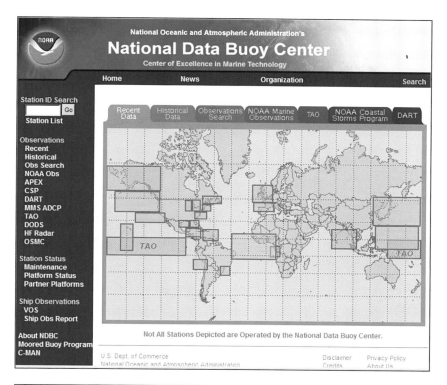

Not All Stations Depicted are Operated by the National Data Buoy Center.

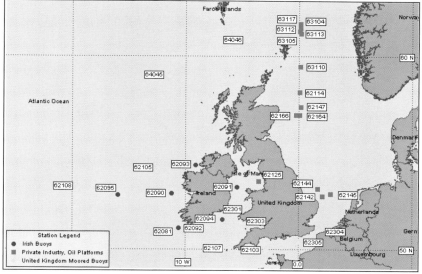

pressure tendency, dew point and wind chill – all vital information for the sailor.

You can also view satellite-derived estimates of the current wind direction and speed (scatterometer readings) by clicking on the relevant links. By selecting "Combined Plot of Wind Speed, Gust and Air Pressure", a page will be displayed showing a graph of all of these elements for the previous 24 hours.

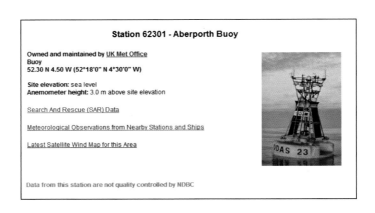

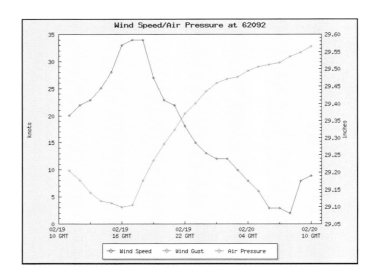

National Hurricane Center (http://www.nhc.noaa.gov)

The National Hurricane Center, provided by the US National Weather Service, is without doubt the best hurricane and tropical storm information and forecast site on the Internet.

Specialist forecasts and analysis charts are provided both for the professional meteorologist and the mariner. Forecasts and information are provided both for the Atlantic and Pacific Oceans. Discussions written by the Hurricane Center forecasters are updated several times a day, as are the high seas forecasts.

There is also an education section which explains why and where hurricanes form and gives advice as to how to avoid them.

During the hurricane season graphical charts are provided which show forecasts of wind speed and the track of tropical storms and hurricanes over the coming days, together with the associated margin of error.

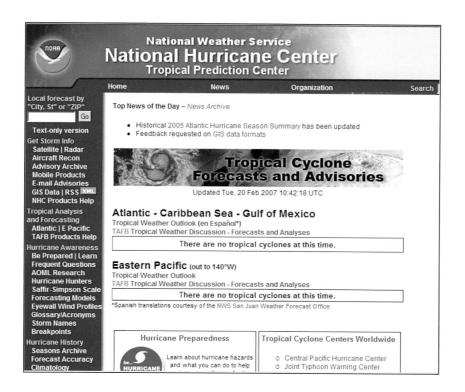

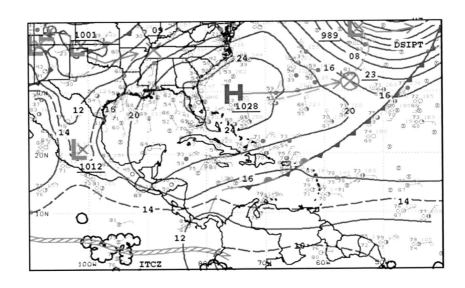

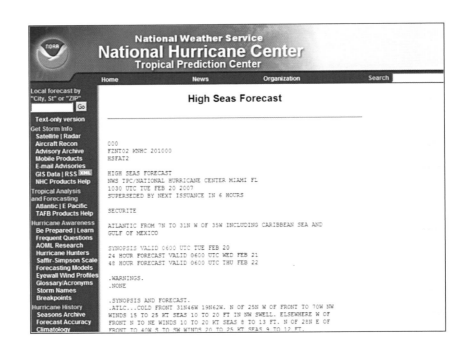

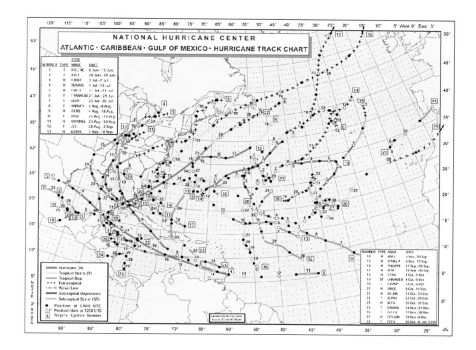

Historical information about hurricanes is contained within the extensive archive maintained on the site. One can find details of hurricane tracks dating back to 1872 as well as information on individual storms. This is invaluable information if you are planning to sail in a hurricane-prone area.

Radiofax, Radioteletype and GRIB

As technology advances, so does the availability of weather information to the sailor whilst at sea. Gone are the days of listening to the Shipping Forecast on longwave and transcribing it in shorthand to be plotted on a chart later (although I have to admit I do still do this, and if you can practice and keep the skill alive it will stand you in good stead).

These days, new innovations are coming along and as satellite communications advance, so will the ability for the sailor to receive vast amounts of information on-board.

I have chosen three technologies to take a look at. Two are rather old now, being radioteletype (RTTY) and HF Radiofax, but when I am asked what weather equipment to take on-board, these are always second after a barometer or barograph. GRIB is a newer technology but one which must be used wisely, as it could present some very dangerous problems for the unsuspecting and inexperienced user.

Radiofax

Let's deal with the old guard first of all. Radiofax has been around for many years now and I still have a deep affection for it. Several weather services still transmit radiofax signals; in Europe the best of these are transmitted from Hamburg and R.N. Northwood.

To receive and view radiofax charts, you will need a shortwave communications receiver (with SSB), an antennae (earthed) and a decoder and

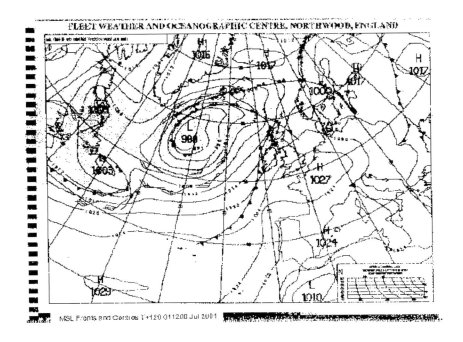

printer. Nowadays the decoder and printer can be replaced by a laptop computer with the necessary software.

I will assume that you are using a laptop computer as this is without doubt the easiest to use on-board. All that is necessary is for you to tune to the appropriate station (see http://www.hffax.de for station and schedule details), connect the radio to the computer and load the decoding software (such as HFFax or JVFax, to name but two).

It's best to practice on-land first to get used to how the signals sound and what information is available. However, before long you will be receiving weather charts "live" and if you leave the system switched on the charts will start and stop automatically, so that you collect charts even when you are not on-board or are asleep, for viewing later.

The main disadvantage with radiofax is that shortwave radio is notoriously susceptible to radio interference. I have known signals to disappear completely for a day or two because of a solar outburst, and this could be most frustrating if you were on-board. However, the advantages outweigh this disadvantage and so I would always recommend having the facility available.

You might like to try a couple of stations. For Hamburg, tune to 3855 kHz, 7880 kHz or 13882.5 kHz. For R.N. Northwood, tune to 2618.5 kHz, 4610 kHz, 8040 kHz or 11086.5 kHz.

Radioteletype

Another rather old-fashioned method of reception of data is to use radioteletype (RTTY). The method of reception is very similar to radiofax in that a shortwave radio (with SSB) is connected to a printer, although now more commonly a laptop computer is used with the appropriate software.

By tuning the radio into the correct station (in Europe the best one is that operated by the German Weather Service) one can get weather reports and forecasts from around the Continent.

Many of the reports are coded (known as SYNOP reports); I won't go into the use of these here. However, there are also forecasts in six-hour time steps for the waters of Europe, extending to five days ahead. These can be invaluable and are repeated every three hours.

The frequencies for the broadcasts are 4583 kHz, 7646 kHz and 10100.8 kHz. It's worthwhile tuning in and becoming familiar with the sound of the broadcasts.

GRIB

You don't need me to tell you that technology moves fast. One of the latest innovations in weather forecasting is the availability of GRIB data. GRIB (GRIdded Binary) is a simple method of transmitting the raw output from the global computer models. This is then decoded by a piece of software on your laptop, and then displayed on the screen as wind, pressure and rainfall information. Forecasts are available up to 14 days ahead.

Sounds marvellous doesn't it? Well, let me sound a note of caution. When using GRIB the sailor must be extremely careful. As this is the raw model output

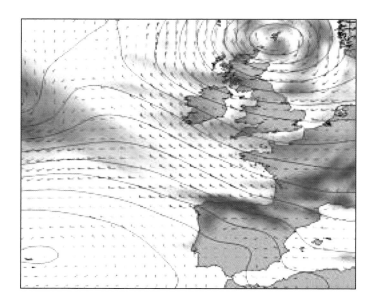

from the global computer models, it has not been amended by a human forecaster. There are times when a computer model can go wrong. I can cite several occasions when if one had relied purely on a GRIB forecast, a dangerous situation would have ensued – on one occasion in September 2006, the GFS GRIB was forecasting a mean wind speed of 15 knots off southwest England, when the actual speeds were nearer 70 knots!

So, with this caveat in place, what do you need to receive GRIB? Well, first, a computer with a method of receiving GRIB files. This could be by email or direct download from a Web site. You then need a type of software to decode the information (called a GRIB viewer). Several free GRIB viewers are available. You then download the weather data file into the viewer and display the maps on your computer. Forecasts can then be stepped ahead, usually in three-hour increments to three days ahead, although as I mentioned earlier, as far ahead as 14 days is available.

I recommend that you visit a few Web sites to learn more. I would suggest:

http://www.grib.us: Register and get a free GRIB viewer and data

http://www.sailmail.com: Receive GRIB files by email

http://www.franksingleton.clara.net: Lots of information about GRIB

Conclusion

I hope that you feel inspired to do more reading into the subject of weather, and that you feel a little more competent in producing your own forecasts. As with so much in life, forecasting is as much about confidence as it is skill; if you make a forecast and it goes wrong, don't be afraid to try again the next day.

I could go on and on, but you would end up with a book so heavy that you would need to get it weighed at a weigh bridge before transporting it. There are many more aspects of the weather which I would like to tell you about, but those will have to wait until the next book.

As a taster, these topics include upper air meteorology. I'd like to explain to you about skew-t and tephigrams, what information they contain (cloud bases,

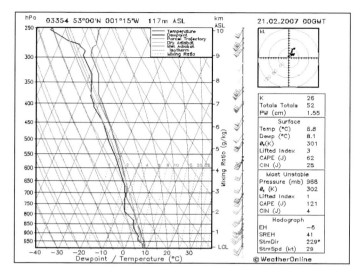

A skew-t diagram

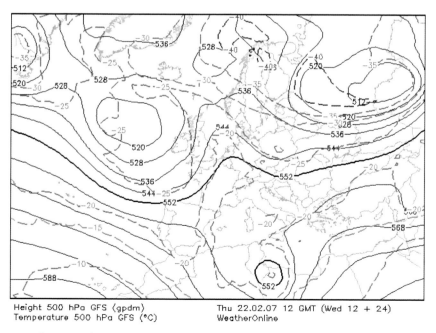

Height 500 hPa GFS (gpdm)
Temperature 500 hPa GFS (°C)

Thu 22.02.07 12 GMT (Wed 12 + 24)
WeatherOnline

An upper-air forecast chart

heights, shower onset times, fog temperatures) and how to use them. Forecast skew-t's are now available on the Internet and so you can predict for yourself how unstable the atmosphere is.

I'd also like to show you some upper air charts and discuss how the sailor can use these charts to make a link between surface and upper air weather patterns. From these charts you can predict how quickly low pressure will form, where gales are likely, and how heavy rain is going to be. But these, and many other things, will have to wait for now. I do hope that the preceding pages have been useful for you and that you are now a weather anorak — just like me! Thanks for reading.

Further Learning at Weather School

If your weather curiosity has been pricked by this book, why not come along to Weather School to find out more?

Weather School runs courses throughout the year for sailors of all abilities and are designed to enhance your weather knowledge, whether you are a novice or expert sailor.

The course aims are to go beyond the information given in the RYA syllabus and bring weather to life for all sailors.

Here's what others who attended Weather School have said:

"Excellent, well worth attending, I learnt a lot. Simon was really good. I came to the course as a complete novice sailor. I have virtually no training in weather or any aspect of it. My knowledge is limited to reading and trying to understand the shipping and inshore waters forecast via Navtex, TV and the internet. I have bought books on the subject, but found them all really hard and so gave up. Although the course was a little advanced for a complete novice, I did understand 75% of the total content and so a course more 'dumbed down' for the beginner wouldn't work. . . . Simon said at the beginning that we may not understand everything but we should learn something from the course, and come out knowing more than when we went in — TRUE! Excellent value for money and I would certainly recommend the course to others."
Martin Pentony-Woolwich, sailor

"Simon's delivery is both easy to understand and enjoyable. Any recreational sailor whose understanding of the weather is, at best, vague would benefit hugely from this

course. Any sailor whose ability to navigate is equal their understanding of weather would also benefit from attending. As a commercial pilot, meteorology is a way of my working life, and I still came away from this course having learnt something, so there is something in it for everyone!!"
Barbara, pilot and sailor

"Thanks for a really interesting and informative day yesterday. I personally got a great deal out of it and it fleshes out the RYA bits nicely. The level of detail, insights into a weatherman and the humour were just right. A great day!"
Richard Stafford, sailor

"Hi Simon, just to say thanks for an excellent day on Saturday. It's nice to meet someone really passionate about weather, I enjoyed it immensely – well done!! Cheers, Jerry."

Check out the Web site at http://www.weatherschool.co.uk for the latest date and course information.

Appendix: Charts for You to Draw

The following pages contain surface-plotted weather charts for you to have a go at analysing yourself. There are no restrictions on photocopying these charts, so do keep on going until you feel you have drawn the chart to your satisfaction.

The charts are in their raw form and so some of the observations may be incorrect. The most frequent errors occur in reports from ships, so if you draw the isobars and find that you can't make them fit due to an observation that looks in error, ignore that observation for the time being and come back to it later. If again you cannot make the observation fit the pressure pattern, discard that observation.

The plots are made using an excellent programme called Digital Atmosphere, available from http://www.weathergraphics.com.

To see how successful you have been, visit http://www.wetterzentrale.de/ topkarten/tkfaxbraar.htm to view the official UK Met Office analysis chart for each day. I haven't included them here because I want you to become familiar with using the Internet for this. Don't forget, though, that an analysis is simply your interpretation of conditions. It will probably not match exactly, although the isobars should be consistent. Frontal positions may be a little different.

Good luck!

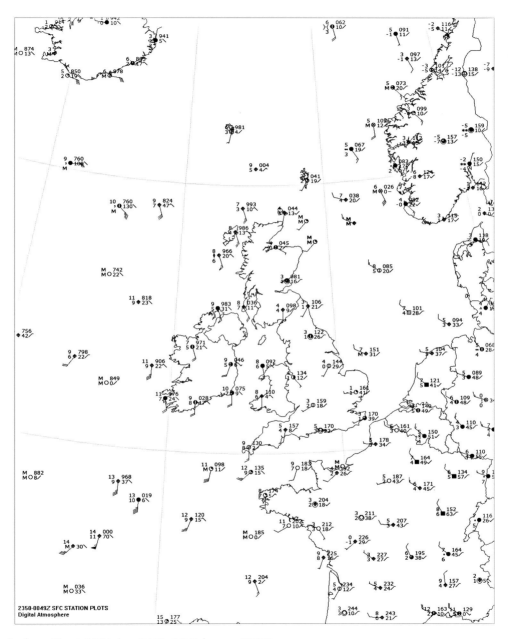

2350-0049Z SFC STATION PLOTS
Digital Atmosphere

Surface Chart 0001 hrs GMT, 15 February 2007

141

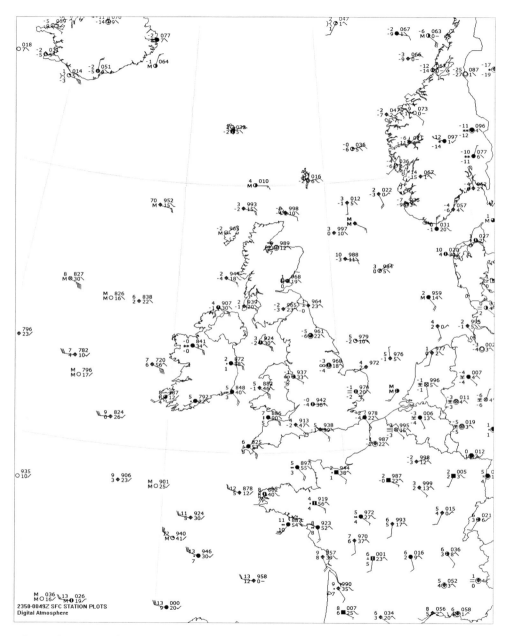

Surface Chart 0001 hrs GMT, 8 February 2007

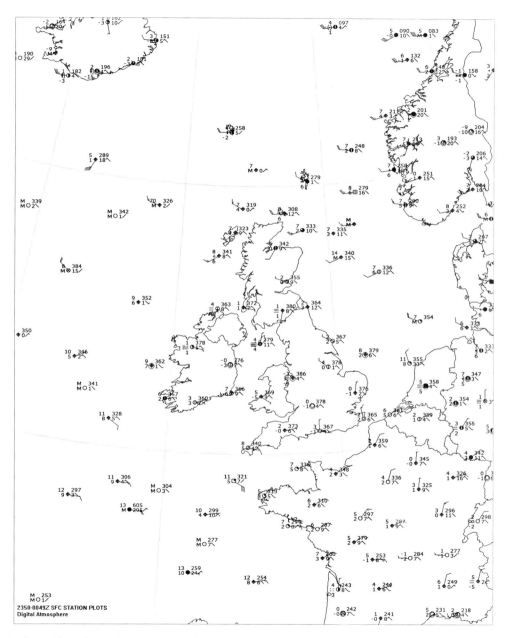

2350-0049Z SFC STATION PLOTS
Digital Atmosphere

Surface Chart 0001 hrs GMT, 4 February 2007

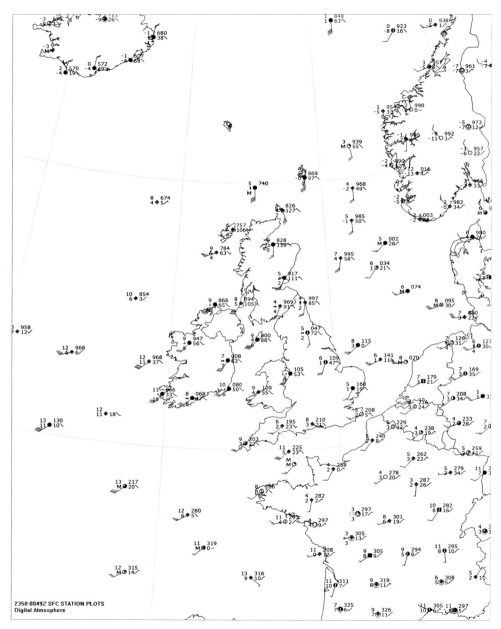

Surface Chart 0001 hrs GMT, 11 January 2007

144

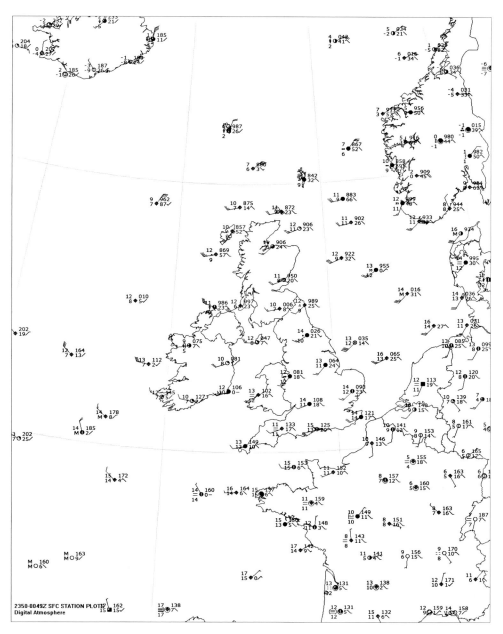

Surface Chart 0001 hrs GMT, 31 October 2006

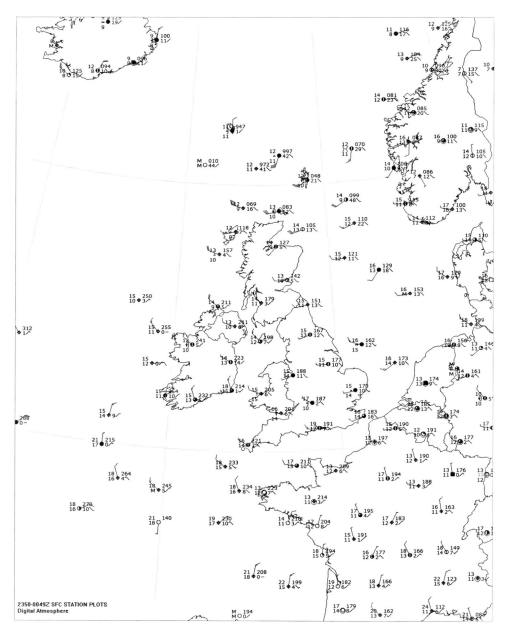

Surface Chart 0001 hrs GMT, 9 August 2006

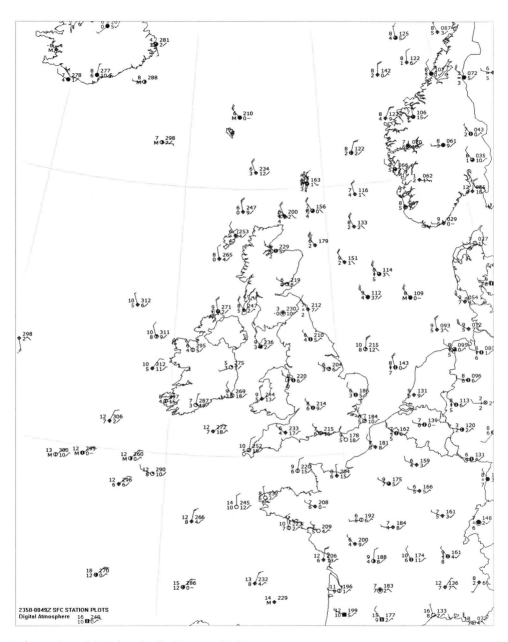

Surface Chart 0001 hrs GMT, 30 May 2006

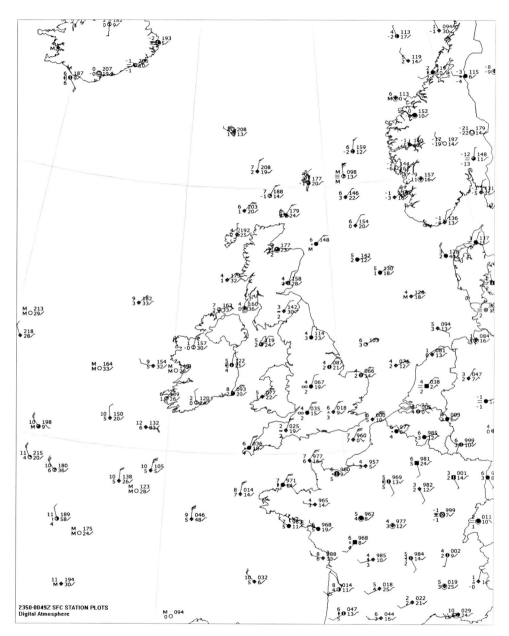

2350-0049Z SFC STATION PLOTS
Digital Atmosphere

Surface Chart 0001 hrs GMT, 20 February 2006

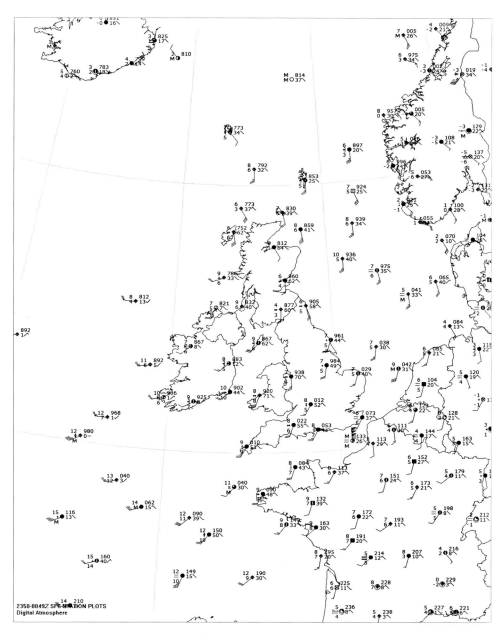

Surface Chart 0001 hrs GMT, 15 February 2006

Index

'Flat calm or force 10. I always wear one.'

Whether they're training or out on a shout, RNLI crew members always wear lifejackets. It's a rule informed by years of experience. They know that, whatever the weather, the sea's extremely unpredictable — and can turn at a moment's notice. They see people caught out all the time. People who've risked, or even lost their lives as a result. The fact is, a lifejacket will buy you vital time in the water — and could even save your life. But only if you're wearing it.

For advice on choosing a lifejacket and how to wear it correctly, call us on 0800 328 0600 (UK) or 1800 789 589 (RoI) or visit our website rnli.org.uk/seasafety/lifejackets

Useless unless worn